More praise for

Black Belt Negotiating

"The principles of Martial Arts have a powerful parallel to the practices in good negotiating. In the next generations, the cultures of Asia will play an increasingly dominant role in world affairs. Michael Soon Lee is an excellent guide to show us not only how to become a master negotiatior, but how to adapt easily to the changes in the world's business culture. Buy this book, read it now, and keep it handy for continued reference. The world is rapidly changing. . . . Are you?"

—Jim Cathcart, author of *The Acorn Principle*

"Becoming a black belt negotiator is much like becoming a fighter pilot. The skills it provides will help you come out on top in any situation. Michael has laid out a flight plan that would have been very valuable to me when I was a CEO. Controlling your emotions and negotiating with integrity and honor are key ingredients to success in business."

—Howard Putnam, former CEO of Southwest Airlines, author of *The Winds of Turbulence*

Black Belt Negotiating

Become a Master Negotiator
Using Powerful Lessons
from the Martial Arts

Michael Soon Lee
with Sensei Grant Tabuchi

AMACOM
American Management Association
New York • Atlanta • Brussels • Chicago • Mexico City • San Francisco
Shanghai • Tokyo • Toronto • Washington, D. C.

Special discounts on bulk quantities of AMACOM books are available to corporations, professional associations, and other organizations. For details, contact Special Sales Department, AMACOM, a division of American Management Association, 1601 Broadway, New York, NY 10019.
Tel: 212–903–8316. Fax: 212–903–8083.
E-mail: specialsls@amanet.org
Website: www.amacombooks.org/go/specialsales
To view all AMACOM titles go to: www.amacombooks.org

This publication is designed to provide accurate and authoritative information in regard to the subject matter covered. It is sold with the understanding that the publisher is not engaged in rendering legal, accounting, or other professional service. If legal advice or other expert assistance is required, the services of a competent professional person should be sought.

Library of Congress Cataloging-in-Publication Data
Lee, Michael Soon.
    Black belt negotiating : become a master negotiator using powerful lessons from the martial arts / Michael Soon Lee ; with Grant Tabuchi.
        p.   cm.
    Includes bibliographical references.
    ISBN 978-0-8144-7461-7
    1. Negotiation in business.   I. Tabuchi, Grant.   II. Title.
    HD58.6.L45   2007
    658.4'052—dc22   2007020972

Printing number

10 9 8 7 6 5 4 3 2 1

CONTENTS

PART V: RED BELT

PART VI: BROWN BELT

PART VII: BLACK BELT

THANKS

Betty Cooper
Frank Furness, CSP
Ian Griffin
John Ho
Ophelia Lopez
Tina Ramirez
Caitlin Williams

My special thanks to editor Amanita Rosenbush in Oakland, California for helping to bring order out of chaos. Also, my eternal gratitude to my loving wife, Miriam, for all of her patience and support in making this book possible.

Finally, my appreciation to Sensei Grant Tabuchi, without whom this book would never have been possible. He certainly has the patience, fortitude, and knowledge of a true black belt.

Martial Arts and the Tao of Negotiating

How would you like an extra $5,000 or $10,000 or more a year to spend? How would you like to have more leisure time? These and more are the benefits of developing exceptional negotiating skills.

How would your life be different if you were a better negotiator? You could be paid more money for your work. You could be driving a nicer car. You could be living in a bigger house. You could be doing more of what you want rather than just automatically complying with what other people ask you to do. Almost everything you have merely been dreaming about could easily become a reality if only you learned the art of strong negotiating.

We have opportunities to negotiate every day, and yet we often fail to get the best possible deal. Studies show that most people believe they could do better when bargaining. This is true not just for the more obvious activities such as asking for a raise or buying a house, but also for issues that do not involve money at all. Who does the dishes at your house? What movies will the family see? Who takes out the garbage? Who drives the kids to school? Who walks the dog? Where will we go out for dinner? All these issues were negotiable at some point. Most of us just give in without question on such issues, and some of us resent the inequality but don't know what to do about it.

So what does negotiating have to do with martial arts? I am an American and proud of it. My great-grandfather came to the United States from Canton, China, in 1855. As an Asian American professional speaker who helps people become better negotiators, I've had the opportunity to travel to many countries and wouldn't choose to live anywhere else in the world.

While growing up in a tough part of Oakland, California, in the 1960s and 1970s, I was literally a 90-pound weakling who was always afraid that some bully would take my lunch or my bicycle. Out of desperation, I bought a set of iron weights, developed a workout regimen, and began studying jujitsu and judo. My new physical strength and budding knowledge of martial arts gave me an exhilarating feeling of confidence.

Eventually, I bought a set of padded mats and turned my father's garage into a *dojo* (school), where I began to teach my friends how to defend themselves against schoolyard bullies. It made me proud when they started calling me *sensei* (teacher), and it gave me a tremendous sense of accomplishment to see them gain skill and confidence.

Even after studying for over forty years and earning black belts in several disciplines, I still have much to learn about martial arts. Today, my teacher is Sensei Grant Tabuchi, a fourth-generation Japanese American who grew up in the San Francisco Bay area, as I did.

Grant is a very interesting and principled man who became attracted to martial arts when he was only six years old by watching Bruce Lee movies. He convinced his parents to let him take basic karate classes at the YMCA, and then he started working with a second-degree black belt teacher who spent an hour and a half every week helping him become stronger and learning a prescribed set of techniques called *katas*. Eventually, he attended a martial arts school owned by Paul Sharp in Fremont, California, where Grant studied tae kwon do. When Paul retired, Grant took over the school and focused his teachings primarily on women and children.

My son Christopher started taking classes from Grant in 1992, and I grew to appreciate the teacher's discipline and dedication to martial arts. This is why I asked Sensei Tabuchi to collaborate with me on this book.

I have been a professional negotiator for over thirty years. During this time, I have had the opportunity to be involved in putting together major motion picture distribution deals, multi-million-dollar real estate transactions, the purchase of dozens of new and used cars, reduced federal income tax bills for clients, and I have even arranged for discounts on gas for my car. Oddly enough, I owe the secret of my success as a negotiator to my martial arts experience.

How? As I was presented with opportunities to negotiate, it occurred to me that they and the martial arts have many aspects in common. A list of these similarities includes the necessity of doing thorough research before entering a contest, the use of leverage, the need to focus all your energies, the importance of timing and balance, the necessity for training and discipline, and much more. These elements can give you a fighting chance at the bargaining table.

I have been applying martial arts principles to the art of negotiating for decades, thus saving both me and my clients hundreds of thousands of dollars. In this book I am going to share my techniques to help you become a winning black belt negotiator. This information will give you the ability to negotiate with increased confidence and success.

This book employs a number of examples involving real estate and car sales. The reason for this is twofold: First, I have been a real estate agent and broker for over thirty years and owned a new-car brokerage company. My experiences in these industries have provided me with a lot of stories. However, the main reason I use real estate and car sales as examples is that they are the two most commonly negotiated items in the United States, Canada, England, France, Germany, Switzerland, and other places where people don't negotiate much else. If you haven't bought a car or a house yourself, you most certainly know someone who has and can relate to these stories.

Using the information in this book to become a black belt negotiator will give you the potential to accumulate sufficient money not only to buy many cars and houses but also to have everything else you want in life. Life is about working hard, but just as important is the ability to negotiate skillfully at every opportunity!

PART I

White Belt

*White signifies the beginning for the new seed.
The students are full of hope and all they need are the
right elements for the seeds to grow to their full potential.*

T he martial arts use nature as a metaphor. As with the pine tree, the seed must be planted and nourished to develop strong roots. Each belt color signifies a stage the seed reaches as it grows to its full potential. Although belt colors may vary slightly from discipline to discipline, the most common are white, yellow, green, blue, red, brown, and black.

The black belt indicates that the wearer has reached the highest possible level of skill. According to legend, there was originally only one color of belt in martial arts—white. Over time, the belt would become soiled and eventually turned black with use, verifying that the student had invested many hours gaining experience. In most disciplines there are ten degrees of black belt, with the tenth degree being the highest.

It is the students' first class, and the teacher enters and welcomes everyone with a bow. From now on, the school is called a *dojo* and the teacher is called the *sensei*. The master shows the students how to wrap the belts around their own waists and tie them so the ends are the same length because the symmetry symbolizes balance, not only in martial arts but in their lives as well. Just as with lessons, this action must be repeated until perfection is achieved. Certain rules must be memorized and followed throughout the students' training—for example, respecting the sensei and the dojo and never using martial arts to show off or impress others.

The first lessons new students learn are how to stand in the most balanced way (if they get it wrong, the sensei will be able to push them over with a single finger) and the rudimentary skill of blocking a punch. Many new students wish they would be taught punches first, but they quickly learn that if they can block properly they will never have to strike. Defense is a better strategy than offense.

As with martial arts, negotiating is an ancient art. In the first chapter of the white belt part of this book, "Modern Lessons from an Ancient Tradition," beginners learn to crawl before they can walk, walk before they can run, and run before they can fly. White belts must forget everything they think they know and learn a whole new system for bargaining more effectively.

In the second chapter, "Overcoming Fear of the Blow," readers must face their fears. New martial arts students hear that they're going to be hit, thrown, kicked, or punched and wonder, "Can I do this? Will I get hurt? Will I embarrass myself?" They also feel anxiety because they are facing the unknown. The white belt symbolizes pure innocence and an empty mind. Each student knows he or she has a lot to learn. The lessons seem familiar, yet they are different, and so it is scary.

Beginning negotiators will also be confronted with their own fears, the most common of which are being rejected or being embarrassed. This chapter will help you learn to overcome those fears and face your opponent with confidence.

In Chapter 3, "Playing to Win," readers find that they aren't just afraid of taking a risk; many don't want to be seen as mean-spirited and hurt their opponents. In other words, they aren't playing to win. Sensei Tabuchi says, "You must go into every contest being focused on winning because your opponent is doing just that. Don't worry about them because they sure aren't worried about you."

Many westerners have been taught the win-win philosophy, which Chapter 3 exposes as a myth. Fighters and negotiators alike must enter the ring expecting to win—or they won't. Bargainers have to keep boring in without giving any quarter, or they'll never reach the black belt stage.

1

Modern Lessons from an Ancient Tradition

For thousands of years, martial arts knowledge and skills have been proven to help seemingly defenseless and weaker underlings defeat much more powerful opponents. Today, people all over the world study them to learn combat skills, physical fitness, self-defense, mental toughness, character development, and self-confidence. Practitioners also develop self-control, concentration, respect, positive character traits, patience, and discipline.

However, the main reason these ancient arts have survived and thrived is their universal connection to spirituality and religions like Buddhism, Taoism, Shinto, and Confucianism. Part of their mystique has always been the apparent contradiction between the violent nature of kicks, blows, and throws and the calm, focused, almost meditative spirit of a martial artist during a contest. The masters of these arts project such a profound presence and execute such remarkable moves that sometimes you have to wonder if they are human like the rest of us.

As we will see, all the qualities cited here can be developed by readers to their great advantage in any bargaining situation. This book examines the secrets of these ancient techniques and reveals how mastering them can give you the power and wisdom it takes to win in a negotiation. These pages contain secrets that will help you uncover your hidden strengths and discover how to leverage them to win over any opponent who does not possess this knowledge, which for years was reserved only for the chosen few. The techniques in this book will also help you uncover your weaknesses and limitations and give you the opportunity to mold yourself into a more formidable opponent.

WONDERS AND BENEFITS

Although westerners might have started practicing martial arts for the physical exercise and self-defense skills, they aren't limited just to these. More men and women are turning to them because of the vast array of health benefits associated with these fitness systems. Here are some of the health benefits that regular practice can bring:

- Increased muscle strength
- Heightened stamina
- Weight loss
- Weight maintenance
- Improved flexibility
- Better posture
- Improved balance
- Enhanced agility

And yet even these are just physical benefits. Martial arts can also work wonders for your mental and emotional well-being, reduce stress, improve concentration, increase self-confidence, and heighten focus. However, increasing numbers of people are drawn to the spiritual principles upon which martial arts are based. As they begin to understand the martial arts, they also begin to understand themselves and other people, as well as the principle that the body, mind, and spirit are inextricably linked. When we are in harmony with the earth's energy, we find balance, strength, and harmony ourselves. Every martial arts style brings with it a unique sense of spirituality.

Spirituality requires you to put your ego aside. As we shall see in future chapters, this is a surprisingly helpful ability in the heat of a negotiation. It might seem that a strong ego would come in handy when you are fighting for what you want, but coming from a clear, objective, and detached egoless state will help you think far more clearly and quickly than your opponent. The more you understand yourself, the less likely you will be to lose your cool. You'll be open to input without the mind censoring or commenting. An ancient Chinese proverb says, "Life is a constant challenge to know oneself." And to know yourself is to know others.

As in poker, a large part of the skill of negotiating is being able to read the person sitting across the table. Some people have a natural knack for it, but whether you do or not, the techniques demonstrated in this book reveal precisely how to interpret your opponent's unconscious behavior and know what he or she is thinking. This might be considered a form of spying, but it is all done in plain view.

THE MARTIAL ARTS AND NEGOTIATING

For most of my adult life I have employed the skills of martial arts in the business world. I have found that my training has been more valuable than the master's degree I earned in business administration. In a sense, the skills involved in karate, kung fu, jujitsu, and other disciplines replicate the art of war. And to a certain degree, winning in business necessitates knowing something about the art of war. On more than one occasion I have thanked my lucky stars for my martial arts experience. It has given me an advantage over many opponents who should have won—but didn't. It is not for nothing that these ancient traditions have survived for century upon century and are more popular today than they ever were. Human beings have always been able to recognize that which is noble, remarkable, and timeless.

Over the years, I have learned that the martial arts are not just a way of life but a way of thinking. The warrior mind-set that martial arts instill enables you to maintain your composure even in extremely stressful situations. The principles apply whether you are sparring with an unknown opponent or negotiating a prenuptial agreement with your significant other. You learn how to control your emotions if you are insulted or belittled by the other party in a negotiation, and you become flexible enough to defend yourself against three opponents at once or to change an entire negotiating team at the last minute. You also learn to make split-second decisions that could have enormous consequences.

As you mature, you learn to rely more on deep thinking over superior strength and brute force. When you're in a contest that goes on for a long time, you will always find the endurance to continue because you will have developed great tenacity. Above all, martial arts will teach you to intensify your focus, while still maintaining a level of calmness, clarity, and intent. As a negotiator, this combination makes you unbeatable.

The spiritual component of martial arts, which permeates all the teachings and lessons, instructs us that negotiators must be in the right state of mind if they wish to navigate all the technical details and emotional land mines that are strewn across a bargaining table.

THIS BOOK

The purpose of this book is to extend the wisdom and the skills of martial arts into the realm of negotiating. The two worlds have certain obvious points in common. Both of them use power and force and have something at stake. In a match or at a bargaining table, you face off with an opponent, you use skill and knowledge, and both sides want to win. These constitute the commonality. In this book, however, you will learn specific techniques from the schools of martial arts that your opponent will not know about. Here are a few of them:

- Developing a strong and powerful stance
- Reading your opponent's mind
- Detecting subtle body cues
- Determining when your opponents are telling the truth and when they are lying
- Getting them to commit first
- Using the art of deception to reach your goals
- Dealing with unethical fighters
- Gaining an advantage over any opponent, no matter how strong
- Determining your opponent's vital striking points
- Leveraging your strengths by learning to strike the right spot
- Overcoming stalemates
- Ending the contest honorably

This book dispels many of the myths that surround the bargaining process, beliefs that keep you from winning the best deal possible. The techniques herein will work not only in business settings but in your personal life.

Negotiating is nothing more than building a relationship between two people, each of whom needs what the other person has. If even the mere thought of haggling makes you nervous, don't worry. With the right knowledge and a little practice, you can improve your skills to such a degree that you will actually look forward to opportunities to bargain.

People who can negotiate well have higher self-esteem and a greater sense of personal power. They know how to spar with their words as much as martial artists spar with their arms and legs. I can think of no other skill that will serve you as well in life.

So why aren't we all better negotiators? When I say the word *negotiate* to people, they usually make a face that looks as if they just bit into a lemon. To most people, bargaining is like taking a tablespoon of bitter medicine—you know you need it, you don't like it, but you feel so good afterward that you're glad you did. If it wasn't so bad after all, why then should one little word stop us in our tracks?

Many people believe that haggling is embarrassing, insulting, or downright rude, except for the big-ticket items like cars and houses. We all have friends who bargain over every purchase, and although we may secretly envy the fact that they save money, we also wish they would stop. We believe that offering less than the sticker price implies that we don't think the seller's goods are worth the price. Or, worse, it looks like we can't afford the item in question, and we consider it undignified to try to bargain the person down. We think we won't be very good at it. We think it won't work. You can add your own personal reasons to this list.

Another major reason people don't ask for a discount is that they're afraid they'll put the vendor out of business. This is nonsense, because if it were true, the seller would never accept your offer. These are experienced businesspeople, so don't insult them by worrying about this. They are very capable of looking out for themselves.

It would simply never occur to most of the people reading this book to walk into a major department store and ask for a discount on some very nice, yet overpriced, suit or evening gown. For all but the most expensive items, we automatically pay the sticker price because we think we have no other choice.

During my travels I have discovered that people in some countries just seem to be better negotiators than people elsewhere. Are you a good negotiator? If you live in the United States, England, Canada, France, Australia, New Zealand, Switzerland, Belgium, Luxembourg, Austria, South Africa, Germany, or any other industrialized country, probably not. However, if you reside in a less industrialized place like Asia, Latin America, Italy, Turkey, Spain, or the Philippines, bargaining is a way of life.

Great negotiators are not born, they are trained. However, you can see that where you are born can determine your comfort level with bargaining. Why the difference? It's not genetics but simply a matter of time and money. In nonnegotiating countries such as the United States, time is a precious commodity but money is fairly plentiful, so to save time, people will negotiate only for the very largest purchases because it could save them a significant amount of money. In negotiating countries such as Asia and South America, time is relatively plentiful but money tends to be scarce, and this gives people there the desire and the time to bargain for just about everything all day long.

For instance, the 2004 average monthly income of an individual in Luxembourg, the United States, and Germany was $3813, $3156, and $2510, respectively, compared to Mainland China, Honduras, and India at $108, $80, and $52. This means that the average person in India earned only $.32 an hour for a forty-hour workweek! You can see that if someone there can reduce the cost of an item by $5 it is a significant savings, whereas in the more industrialized countries many people would usually not bother to haggle over such a relatively insignificant amount of money.

Different parts of the world use various terms for negotiating. In Canada it's called *bartering*. In England it's known as *haggling*. In America it's just thought of as downright unpleasant. Even when we could save money, we don't negotiate. The Saturn car company is only two decades old, and yet its cars are one of the more popular American brands not because the company promises you the greatest car in the world. What has made Saturn so popular here is the company's negotiating policy, which is—no negotiating! When you ask Saturn dealers who their customers are, you'll find that they're puzzled that very few Asians, Hispanics, or others from negotiating countries buy their product. If, in turn, you ask such car buyers why they don't buy Saturns, you'll discover that they believe they will pay too much money if they can't negotiate the asking price.

In the western world our reluctance to negotiate doesn't hold us back just at the mall but in our personal lives as well. When our college-age kids assert their right to ask us for thousands of dollars just because we share the same last name, we feel obliged to automatically comply. Joey says he needs a new car, so we just hand over the cash.

If you're not used to it, entering into a negotiation can make you feel like little David facing the behemoth Goliath armed with only a tiny slingshot and bad aim. Yet I can assure you, you haven't always felt this way. When you were a child you were likely an excellent negotiator, one of the world's best. You had to be to get what you wanted. After all, you had no real power or money of your own. All you really possessed was a single-minded desire to get your needs met. Children never give up. They know our weak spots and instinctively understand how to exploit them. They will zero in on a toy or a doll and never take their attention off it until they leave the store with it.

I may teach negotiating seminars to thousands of people, but I am not exempt from manipulation by my own children. When my son was very young we went to Disneyland. It was a hot day, and after a couple of sweaty hours he said to me out of the blue, "Daddy, you love me don't you?" Not knowing I was walking into a trap, I quickly replied, "Of course, Christopher, very much." Closing the snare firmly around me, he then said, "If you are really nice to me and buy me an ice cream cone, I'll let you carry me the rest of the day." Well guess who got the ice cream cone and guess who got the bad knees from carrying him all over the amusement park?

Children don't realize that it's not socially acceptable to ask repeatedly for what they want, and so they do. They don't care if they're annoying. After all, their parents can't leave them behind a bush somewhere just because they get on their nerves. In the end, parents usually give in, if for no other reason than just to shut them up.

I am certainly not advocating that you annoy your friends, family, and associates to get what you want. I am, however, admiring the pluck and persistence of children, and sometimes their cunning and creativity. I think that many of us would do well to tap into that spirit. Somewhere along the line we started to feel that we shouldn't bother to work the price down if we could afford to pay what's on the sticker. Also, we bought into the adage that time is money, so to save time we simply pay the price as marked.

This book will debunk many of your beliefs and take the wind out of your fears about negotiating. By following some basic principles that have been used for thousands of years by champion martial artists to hone their craft, you can learn the art of becoming a master negotiator. However, you must be willing to apply these principles out in the real world. Reading about it isn't enough. Even the most successful CEO, nurse, lawyer, salesperson, or teacher who wants to learn martial arts has to walk into the dojo for the first time and assume a fighting stance. You might be nervous, you might feel like the novice that you are, but everyone has to start from the beginning.

WHAT IS NEGOTIATING REALLY ABOUT?

Webster's dictionary defines negotiating as follows: "to confer with another so as to arrive at the settlement of some matter." So what is all the fear about? It is nothing more than talking with another person to come to an agreement that is not only beneficial but satisfactory and fair to both sides. It doesn't mean taking advantage of people or forcing them to do something they don't want to do. You don't need to threaten or coerce. You don't have to lie or cheat. You can and should form an honorable and honest relationship with your opponent so both of you can get your needs met.

Professional negotiators know that bringing two parties together who both want a fair agreement can be a very satisfying experience. It certainly doesn't have to be unpleasant or stressful. There is no need to use force because the self-interest of each side is enough to bring about a successful conclusion. Both parties agree because it's in their best interests to do so and for no other reason.

In martial arts, there is a code of honor that varies from discipline to discipline but usually contains the following basic principles:

1. Respect your school.
2. Respect your teacher.
3. Respect your fellow students.
4. Honor your opponents.
5. Fight fairly.

Likewise, there is a code of honor among professional negotiators. Its tenets may not be recorded in a manual somewhere, but everyone knows what they are:

1. Respect the negotiating profession.
2. Respect your opponent.
3. Be honest.
4. Give your best effort.
5. Negotiate fairly.

Following these principles is not only a moral choice but a practical one as well: It helps build trust so that an agreement that works for all the parties can be reached. It might take a few minutes, hours, weeks, months, or even years, but in the end, both parties are satisfied. It can be seen as a great tool for relationships, society, and the culture at large because it is a way of helping people resolve conflicts in a civilized fashion. How many wars could be avoided if people knew how to treat each other courteously?

NEGOTIATING IS NOT BEGGING

One important piece of information you will take away from this book is that there is a big difference between negotiating and begging. A man called my office one day and said to my assistant, "I want to attend Michael Lee's negotiating seminar, but I don't want to pay the regular price of a hundred and ninety-nine dollars. I only want to pay ninety-nine." My staff person, who is quite well trained, said, "Why should we give you a hundred-dollar discount?" He responded, "Well, it's a negotiating class and I'm negotiating." My assistant then just repeated the price of the program, at which point the gentleman hung up.

Unfortunately, we never heard from the caller again, because he really could have used the course! He wasn't negotiating, he was begging, which is asking for something for nothing. Negotiating, in contrast, means helping people get what they want so they feel willing to give you what you want. What might this gentleman have done for us that would have compelled us to give him a discount? He could have reduced our marketing costs by offering to bring other people to my program. He could have assisted us with registration at the event, which would have saved us the cost of another staff person. There are many ways he could have *earned* a discount, but that would have required him to first think, "What's in it for them?" rather than just "What's in it for me?" I will teach you the critical importance, if you want to win, of putting yourself in your opponent's shoes first.

ON GENDER

This book was written as much for women as for men. Why? Because women need money and they need a good deal just as much as any man. Yet research shows that they are far more reluctant to bargain or fight for what they want. Just look in the average home for proof. There might be no absolutes about gender roles or division of labor in today's household, yet research shows that women in America still do two-thirds of the housework and most of the child care because they don't see these duties as negotiable. (In other countries the statistics reveal an even greater disparity.) As a result, women have less leisure time and more stress. Obviously, women have to learn to negotiate their roles more effectively in the new husband-wife paradigm.

In their book *Women Don't Ask*, authors Linda Babcock and Sara Laschever contend that women tend to be the weaker sex when it comes to negotiating. They note that females are 2.5 times more likely than men to say that they feel "a great deal of apprehension" about negotiating. As a result, the authors found that women are much less likely than men to ask for what they want or need.

Babcock and Laschever say that women are also less aggressive than men when bargaining. Men initiate negotiations four times more often than women. In fact, 20 percent of women (22 million) say they never negotiate at all, yet they agree that negotiating is appropriate and necessary.

Is it only older women from earlier generations who fall into this trap? Babcock and Laschever say that younger women believe they ask for what they want as much as men. However, after doing the research on younger women in the twenty-first century, the authors found that men are still much more likely to ask.

Additionally, Babcock and Laschever note that not negotiating hurts women financially. By not asking for more than she is offered for her first salary, a woman stands to lose more than $500,000 over the course of a career by the time she's 60. In contrast, men are four times more likely than women to negotiate their first salary. Employers expect prospective employees to negotiate, so they usually offer less than they initially are prepared to pay.

Men also negotiate more throughout their careers, making the difference even larger.

Women need money just as much as men, so why don't they negotiate for higher salaries, too? Because they often lack the self-confidence to do so. This is one of the main reasons that women of all ages are joining martial arts studios in droves—not just for self-defense and exercise but more for the sense of confidence, freedom, and psychological power that it gives them. There are some of the unique traits that women can use to their advantage at the bargaining table. They tend to be more collaborative, which is exactly what is needed to develop complex agreements between diametrically opposing parties. Each party must receive what it wants, or it will not accept the deal. Notice that most girls' games involve cooperation, not competition.

To their advantage, women tend to be more compassionate than men, allowing them to view a transaction from the perspective of the other party. As children, girls are taught to focus on the needs of others, not on themselves. This is what you need to do to bring opposing parties together. Although many men must learn to ask themselves what's in it for the other person, and then practice doing so, most women already possess this attribute instinctively.

As I point out later in the book, in many ways women have tendencies that make them *better* negotiators than men, if only they can identify and use those tendencies. I also show women that areas in which males are typically thought to be dominant—such as being aggressive and obstinate—can often work against men. One thing I do not advocate is telling women that they have to be more like men to be good at bargaining. They can use their natural talents for collaboration, listening, and empathy to win a good deal for themselves. In martial arts, women compete at the same level as men all the time using their own attributes in their own way. Women fighters tend to be quicker, more flexible, and stronger in the legs than men. Once they are aware of these advantages, they can employ them expertly with great success.

I have seen all types of people succeed at martial arts—male, female, short, tall, skinny, fat, young, old, and even people in wheelchairs. Regardless of who you are, this book will provide you with a totally new system—yet, ironically, one that is based on ancient knowledge—for beating opponents who seem to be out of your league. You will discover how, for thousands of years, top martial artists have won matches against overwhelming odds using techniques that can be applied to the bargaining process.

2

Overcoming Fear of the Blow

Fear is only as deep as the mind allows.
ANCIENT JAPANESE PROVERB

Before martial arts students can begin their physical training, they must first learn the mental part of the game. One of the fundamental issues they must face is fear. Martial artists, who cannot be afraid when they step into the ring or it will ruin their career, deal with fear by acquiring knowledge. So can you. One way fighters acquire knowledge is to practice basic kicks and punches, then move up to sparring, and finally progress to tournaments. In other words, they move in stages.

For anyone studying the martial arts, probably the biggest fear is of getting hurt, especially in a full-contact contest where you are actually allowed to hit your opponent. In this kind of venue you could really be injured or even knocked out if you don't have the proper training. In other words, you ought to be afraid if you enter the ring unprepared. So how do martial artists acquire the kind of knowledge that helps them deal with feelings of dread? First, by learning solid techniques that teach them how to block punches and kicks, which gives them a sense of confidence. Second, most teachers will show them how to tighten their stomach muscles to deflect a direct hit or turn slightly to make a blow glance off a vulnerable spot, as well as other techniques. They've learned that by being aggressive and proactive there is less chance of being hurt than if they are merely being defensive. Third, controlled sparring as a green belt shows them what it feels like to be hit lightly. And finally, full-contact sparring as a red belt teaches them what it's like to be hit full force. What they learn from this training is that they can survive blows through a combination of technique and practice. In fact, once you are hit a couple of times, you realize it isn't so bad, and you stop panicking at the thought of a blow.

When you say the word *negotiate*, some people's hearts instantly start racing out of fear. It may not be the kind of fear you feel when you're standing in the middle of an intersection and you look up to see a 10-ton Mack truck careening toward you. But it is the kind of uneasiness that stops you from doing something scary, even though you know you should do it. How many people know they're way overdue for a visit to the dentist, but anxiety keeps them from making an appointment? How many want to ask someone for a favor, and it would probably be fine, yet they can't bring themselves to do it face-to-face? If you think you are one of those people who is *not* afraid of negotiating, then why aren't you doing it more often? Something is holding you back, and it's probably fear.

COMMON FEARS ABOUT NEGOTIATION

Many fears keep people from becoming master negotiators. You might be afraid of the sting of rejection if the other party doesn't accept your offer. You might be afraid that you'll be embarrassed because you think haggling is undignified. You might be afraid to put a company out of business if you ask for a discount. You might fear that the other party will be offended by an offer you make and become angry. These and hundreds of other types of misgivings, real or imagined, keep you and others from putting more money into your pockets every year from everything you buy and sell.

Let's look at the seven most prevalent fears surrounding the bargaining process. First, I have found that the most common reason people don't ask for what they want is that they are afraid of rejection. This is probably the silliest fear of all because in negotiating you really have nothing to lose. Just ask yourself, "What's the worst that can happen if I ask for a discount and the seller says no?" You were paying full price before you asked for a discount and you will still pay full price if they reject your request, so how much worse off are you than before you asked? No worse!

Many of us fear rejection because we feel somewhat powerless when we're asking someone for something and they can turn us down. However, if you ask and they say no, you always have it within your power to do some reject-ing of your own—you can take your business somewhere else. There is always another store, parking lot, restaurant, hair cutter, or dry cleaner. Rarely does anyone have a monopoly on a product or service. However, now that you've asked, the choice is yours. Later I will give you a whole system for practicing your negotiating skills, but you can start small by going to your favorite restau-rant, a place where you eat on a regular basis, where the manager should def-initely give you something off the bill for your continued patronage. In other words, start where you live.

Why on earth would a hair stylist, dry cleaner, or restaurant give you a 10 or 20 percent discount or more? Simply because your loyalty as a customer saves the business at least that much and more in marketing costs. Many smart businesspeople recognize the benefits of attracting and retaining repeat customers by offering a "frequent buyer" discount. For example, a deli I often go to offers a free sandwich after you have purchased ten. The local Chinese restaurant gives a $10 discount for every $100 I spend. The airport parking lot I use gives me five free days after I have parked my car there for thirty days (not necessarily consecutively). The nursery where I buy trees and plants takes $10 off after I have spent $100. To keep me coming back, the office supply company I patronize gives me a rebate on every dollar I spend. The airport limousine company I use gives me a free ride after I have paid for six. And on it goes. Obviously, I don't ask for a discount at these places, because they already reward me for being a loyal customer. What businesses do you deal with that don't?

Aspiring negotiators can deal with their fears by practicing wherever they go. It's best to start with small, inexpensive items and then work your way up to bigger purchases. If a business that you patronize doesn't have an official incentive program, you can make up your own by having the salesperson ini-tial the back of the company's business card every time you come in, or just remind the salesperson that you are entitled to the *frequent buyer discount.*

Another common excuse for why people don't negotiate is that they're afraid to appear undignified. If saving thousands of dollars a year seems some-how vulgar or crass to you, then simply pay full price for everything you buy and you'll never have your dignity offended. I think that an integral part of this excuse is that people don't want to look like they're poor or that they need the extra money a discount would provide. It's an interesting fact that the very richest people are the most conscious of every dollar they spend. How do you think they became rich? They have learned to control their money and will ask for a discount every chance they get. So instead of being afraid of looking poor, ask for a price reduction the way the rich do.

Another reason I often hear people give for not negotiating is that they just don't think it's worth the effort. My wife and I eat out at a nice restaurant once or twice a week, and rarely do we pay full price. In fact, we usually get half off, saving us at least $20 a week, well over $1,000 a year, on restaurant food alone. Add to this the amount that improved negotiating skills could save you on such things as laundry, hair styling, health club memberships, credit card interest, movie tickets, jewelry, clothing, office supplies, and thousands of other items. What would you do with an extra $1,000 to $5,000 a year or more? If you don't want to spend it on yourself, could you use it for your children or give it to your favorite charity? Also, don't forget that this is after-tax savings. Most people in industrialized countries pay between 30 and 50 percent in income taxes. This means that to have $1,000 to $5,000 a year to spend after taxes you had to earn about $2,000 to $10,000 before taxes. Now does it seem worth the trouble to negotiate?

The fourth most common reason I've heard for why people don't bargain is that they're afraid they might actually put a company out of business. Upon closer examination, you can see the fallacy of this concern. Store owners are usually very sophisticated businesspeople who should be aware of their incomes, costs, and profit margins. If someone is asking for goods or services at a price that would result in a loss to them, they won't do it. If they agree to your offer of a discounted price, you can rest assured they are still making money off the deal.

One extremely common reason that many people show a fear of negotiating is that they don't want to take risks. Sensei Tabuchi has found in the dojo that men tend to take more risks than women. For example, guys will regularly choose very difficult boards to break. He finds women to be more thoughtful and conservative when it comes to risk.

The sixth reason more of us don't negotiate is an unusual one: Negotiating isn't part of our identity. If I suggest that you try to work out a better deal on dinner at a restaurant that you go to all the time, and you find yourself saying, "Oh, I could *never* do that," then that is an indication that negotiating isn't part of your identity. Most of us have no idea what our identity consists of until it is challenged. "I could never . . . ," "That isn't me . . . ," and "I just can't see myself . . ." are phrases that are indications that a certain activity is outside our identity. All of us see ourselves fundamentally as a certain *kind of person*, that that kind of person will do only certain *kinds of things*. Perhaps other people could manage this alien activity, but not you. If, for example, you were raised as a nice Southern belle, you probably wouldn't be able to imagine yourself getting into a shouting match with someone over a taxi. But a native New Yorker would likely do it in a heartbeat.

Identity is our core picture of who we are, and it is central to our lives. People live and die because of it, and it can cause severe limitations if we won't step outside of it. If you shudder at the thought of haggling for a better deal for yourself because "it's just not me," then you need to stretch your whole idea of yourself. Do it in small increments. As I mentioned, start small and work your way up from there. You might actually find it liberating to occasionally challenge your identity.

When you start taking a martial arts class, you are required to have a *Gi*, or uniform, consisting of a jacket, pants, and a white belt. This uniform stamps you with the identity of a martial artist. Unfortunately, there are few readily identifiable accessories associated with negotiating that could give you that kind of recognizable persona. There are, however, a few techniques that will help you identify with strong negotiators:

- Glue two quarters together with both heads facing out to remind you that in negotiations you can never lose. Tossing them in the air will help you decide whether you should ask for a deal. (Heads you will, and tails you won't.)
- Write out and post support affirmations such as "I negotiate with confidence" or "I am a powerful negotiator" in conspicuous locations, such as on your bathroom mirror and your refrigerator door.
- Write out and post mirror and match affirmations such as "I notice the physical stance and energy of my opponent" or "I mirror the physical stance and energy of my opponent" in conspicuous locations, such as above your computer monitor and at your desk. This will remind you to mirror and match your opponent's body language, rate of speech, and energy, as explained in Chapter 9.
- Cut out and make copies of the Needs and Wants Sheet that you will find in the appendix of this book, which should be completed before every negotiation.

- When you have completed this book, cut out and carry with you the black belt negotiating Certificate of Completion in the appendix. It certifies that you have acquired the skills and completed all the tests to become a black belt negotiator.

Just as beginning martial artists start practicing their craft very slowly and safely, you will begin to manifest your intention of becoming a powerful negotiator by starting with very low risk negotiation tactics, and belt after belt you will improve your skills.

Tens of thousands of people join martial arts studios every year. Countless others have the intention to start yet never do. Among the excuses I've heard are "I'm too young," "I'm too old," "I'm too short," "I'm too tall," "I'm too fat," "I'm too skinny," "I'm too clumsy," and hundreds of other *too*'s. Yet if you go to any martial arts school, you will see people of every description enjoying the various activities. Clearly, those who are still spectators haven't identified the real reason for not trying something new.

There are endless excuses people give for why they don't bargain for items they want; it's mostly because they're afraid to examine their reservations. Often, they don't even know what they're afraid of. If you can identify the fears that are holding you back, there is no reason you can't become a black belt negotiator yourself. Great martial arts instructors bring their students' fears out into the open, and then they find that those fears quickly lose their power. In the cold light of day, they're just not that scary.

Let's look at some general principles that can help you overcome the fears associated with bargaining.

PRINCIPLES OF OVERCOMING FEAR

Experienced martial arts instructors help white belts overcome fear by allowing them to experience success very early in their training. You wouldn't want to have newbies out there trying to break bricks during their first lesson; they would never come back for a second. Instead, you give them plastic practice boards they can easily break and then move them up to soft pine boards. This gives them faith in their technique and confidence in their teacher. Eventually they will graduate to harder boards and then to thin bricks. All the while, their technique is improving at the same time their confidence is growing. Eventually, they can increase the thickness of the bricks to an impressive level.

In the same way, the more you practice bargaining, the more comfortable you will be with it and with all the possible outcomes. We all have fears, especially when embarking on something that is new and different. After a short time, though, if you face them and manage them, the fears lose their power to control you, and you begin to control the fears.

Having said that, a little fear is actually a good thing. Even the most experienced fighters feel some hint of uneasiness before going into the ring. It keeps them sharp and alert. One other point: The fear of failure drives them to properly prepare before a tournament. Sensei Tabuchi says, "Nerves are good because they keep you aware." The trick is to channel nervousness into positive energy, which is what I do on the platform every time I'm speaking to a large audience. There is a fine line between panic and excitement. Learn to turn the toxic energy of panic into the creative energy of excitement, and you can conquer the world.

Ironically, many women are much more afraid of winning than they are of losing, not because they don't want the gains, but because they are reluctant to turn the other party into a loser and create hard feelings. They are also afraid of being labeled pushy, aggressive, or overly ambitious. They're afraid of not acting like society's image of a lady. Women might know how to fight for their children, but they won't expend the same energy for pure self-interest. They have to learn to head into a negotiation feeling entitled to win and not leave money on the table when it's over. Many women are far too willing to settle for scraps or incremental wins, and they shy away from scoring big in a negotiation. By holding back, they compromise their goals and undermine their own needs before the bargaining ever begins. Perhaps women need to get in touch with their masculine side, the part that knows they deserve to walk away with as big a piece of the pie as they can.

The best way to overcome the fear of taking risks is, again, to take small steps. Martial artists always practice risky techniques, such as breaking boards, in a safe venue first. They start at home, then move to their own dojo, and finally go to tournaments that are open to the public. If you are afraid of being embarrassed, start by negotiating with a business owner you know well and then move on to companies you are not as familiar with.

Martial artists often have a prefight routine to steady themselves. Negotiators can calm their nerves by having a well-rehearsed opening line. Many experienced buyers will have a set way of complimenting sellers on whatever items they are selling. In real estate, it's sometimes hard to find something nice to say about a house, so I might start by saying, "The way you've decorated your home is so interesting." The seller always takes this as a compliment, and it starts off the talks on a positive note.

The biggest fear of all is losing. What if you took the edge off that type of dread by seeing that losing isn't the end of the world? Many martial artists go into a contest looking not to win but just to gain experience. If all you are looking to do is learn something, you can't lose. This is an especially valuable approach when you just begin practicing your craft, because the chances of your coming out with a big win are small. However, you learn that the experience you gain with every loss brings you just a bit closer to a victory.

If you want to sell or buy something and you're afraid even to try because your efforts might not pay off, you might venture into the transaction with no expectation of walking away with any gains at all except knowledge. This attitude takes the pressure to perform off you, and it lets you enter all kinds of situations you would never have dared to before, just because you have nothing to lose. Keep in mind my cardinal principle: If you ask for a price reduction and the seller says no, you aren't any worse off than before you started. If you never ask, the answer is always no.

Remember: If you don't receive the answer you want, you always have the option to walk away. There is absolutely no commitment until both parties agree, so you don't have to worry about being trapped into a deal you don't want.

Even when you are a proficient negotiator, you will not win every time. But real winners stay in the game even when they hit a losing streak. Their time will come again. The real losers in this world tend to quit after they are defeated one time. Martial artists consider loss as just another lesson on the road to becoming a black belt. Sensei Tabuchi says, "You can't learn if you always win. Losing can teach you some of the most valuable lessons."

One of the biggest benefits of martial arts is the confidence it gives you. The more you accomplish, the higher your self-esteem rises. As you work your way through the material and exercises in this book, your bargaining esteem will increase as well. As you practice your negotiation skills, your confidence will rise and your fear will diminish. However, never expect it to go away completely because it shouldn't. Fear will keep you sharp and motivate you to engage in all the activities necessary to make you successful. For instance, even though I've given thousands of paid presentations all over the world, I still get a few butterflies in my stomach before every speech. If I didn't, I'm sure my performance would suffer because I wouldn't work as hard to make it flawless.

Part of the fears many people experience around negotiating comes from a mistaken need to develop win-win solutions in bargaining. We'll deal with this issue in Chapter 3.

3

Playing to Win

Always negotiate for the best deal you can.
Do not be concerned about fairness,
as long as the other party can protect his
or her own interests.
MICHAEL SOON LEE

Nearly every negotiating book ever written takes a *win-win* approach to agreements. This may come as a shock, but I believe that win-win is for losers. I would submit to you that nobody believes in win-win because people play to win—not to tie, and certainly not to lose.

In martial arts, whether you are sparring for practice or in a tournament, you do not want your opponent to win. Even if the person across the mat from you is your best friend or your brother or sister, you still don't want the person to beat you. There's nothing wrong with this attitude because the need to win is human nature, for both men and women, and it's what drives us to do our best.

But let's be clear—winning doesn't mean breaking even. You wouldn't be interested in playing blackjack in Las Vegas if every hand ended in a push (tie). If your hockey or soccer team ended every game tied, would you consider it a win? If you had a bet on the game, would it pay off? No. Martial artists play to win, and so do you.

Thomas Hobbes, the seventeenth-century philosopher, said that people always act out of their own self-interest. In business, many say that acting in one's own self-interest is the basis for free-market capitalism. Contracts are signed with each party's own interests in mind. The act leading up to the contract is the negotiation, and the winning attitude must start there. This is not to say that the opposing party does not get what he or she wants out of a deal as well, but an experienced negotiator lets the other person have it on the negotiator's own terms. The mark of black belt negotiators is to walk away from the table with what they came for while letting their opponents *feel* they got a good deal as well. Now *that's* skill.

Win-win suggests a tie wherein you, in the best-case scenario, end up with a dissatisfying compromise. Alternatively, when you leave everyone happy, it means you got what you came for while still making sure the other party's needs were met. I suggest that you follow more of an "everyone's happy" philosophy.

When you truly win, it means all your needs were met and you obtained as many of your wants as possible. Chapter 6 discusses how to recognize the difference between wants and needs and how to keep them at the front of your mind.

Too many people feel guilty if they win big by obtaining more of what they want from a deal than their opponents seem to. Don't fall into that trap. They aren't going to agree to any deal in which you are the only one to benefit. For all you know, they may be going through a divorce, job transfer, or illness; they may need cash; they may have tax problems, or they may be experiencing some other situation that you are helping them resolve. There was a story in the newspaper a few years back about a man who was running off with his secretary after telling his wife he wanted a divorce. Before he left town to vacation with his new sweetheart, he hastily called his wife and told her to sell his Mercedes for as much as she could get and send him the money in the Bahamas. She sold the brand-new car for $1. Now, the buyer of that Mercedes definitely got a good deal, but he needn't have felt bad. The wife found immeasurable satisfaction in sending her ex-husband a check for a single dollar.

There could literally be a hundred reasons why someone wants to buy or sell, the fairness of which is not our concern. The only reason to find out is that it could give us negotiating leverage. Don't forget that the other party could feel he or she is the winner and getting the deal of a lifetime from you. Again, the other party's gain is not your concern.

Bargain with your own interests in mind, and assume the other party will do the same. My family had some large items cluttering up our garage, so we asked a hauling company to come over to give us an estimate. After looking at the freezer, file cabinets, and other assorted pieces of furniture, they quoted us $275. I told them we would have to think about it and reminded them that if they had to come back, it would cost them time and money for gas. At that point, they offered to drop the price to $175. I stalled, suggesting that we might call in a nonprofit group that would gladly accept some of the items and take them away for free. After a little more back-and-forth, the supervisor actually asked me what I would be willing to pay for the hauling, to which I offered $100. We eventually settled for $110 because the momentum was in my favor.

The principle here is this: Always negotiate for the best deal you can for your side. Do not be concerned about fairness as long as the other party can protect his or her own interests. So how does this fit the principle? In the aforementioned hauling example, I was prepared to pay at least $150—the minimum cost of having to do the job myself—so I believe that I won big. However, the hauling company does not have to pay the $50 dump fee that I would have been charged because it pays by the truckload, which includes the refuse of a lot of other people besides me. The hauling company's cost for my share was probably about $20. It still netted $90, which meant the company won a little as well. Certainly this was not a *win-win* but more of an *everyone's happy* result.

Although you don't *have to* take into consideration the other party's motivation, it helps you negotiate more effectively if you at least know what it is. For one thing, you can estimate how motivated the other person is. (For help with this, use some of the techniques in this book such as spying on your opponent, discussed in Chapter 5.) However, it's difficult to know exactly what another person is thinking. On the one hand, the person may have expected to receive less for something he or she is selling or pay more for something he or she is buying. On the other hand, the person may be in dire need of what you have to sell or the money derived from what you are buying.

This principle is especially important for women to embrace. In *Women Don't Ask*, Babcock and Laschever say, "Women's strong urge to foster and protect relationships can make many of them fear that a disagreement about the outcome of a negotiation—a disagreement about the issues being discussed— actually represents a personal conflict between the negotiators involved." They often value collaboration over winning.

In fact, women want to win just as much as men. I've seen a group of women get together for a "friendly" game of cards, and they start out by saying, "Let's just have fun and it doesn't matter who wins." Later I hear them yelling at each other, "You can't do that!" or "That point was mine!" I'm thinking, "If it doesn't matter who wins, why do you care so much?" It's human nature to want to win.

Yet women do approach negotiating differently from men. Males tend to act like lions on the African savannah. When they kill another animal they rip off the biggest piece of meat they can; they have no intention of leaving empty-handed. Females are often more like birds of prey, which wait for a chance to pick at what's left over. Women must recognize that they are entitled to just as big a piece of the prize as males and then train themselves to ask for it.

In both martial arts and negotiating, other people's circumstances and mind-set are of little concern to a negotiator unless they fall into an area of taking unfair advantage of them. In martial arts you are taught to never attack an opponent who is injured or otherwise helpless. The same rules apply when negotiating. For example, I once explained to the owner of a lovely home in a desirable neighborhood that homes similar to hers in the area were currently selling for around $400,000. This sweet elderly lady smiled at me and said, "Oh no, honey, that's way too much. I only paid thirty thousand dollars for this house fifty years ago and couldn't take more than one hundred thousand for it today."

Many people to whom I have related this story have told me that I should have bought the house myself for the $100,000 she wanted and then turned around and resold it for a $300,000 profit. First, there are a number of real estate laws and Realtor codes of ethics that prohibit exactly this kind of "secret profit." Second, I could never, in good conscience, take advantage of someone like this.

In this case my instincts told me that the seller was not in complete control of her mental faculties because what homeowner doesn't want to maximize his or her sales price? It turned out that my gut feeling was correct, because shortly after I explained the situation to the seller's family, they had her institutionalized. I then sold the property at fair market value, which helped take care of her living expenses in the rest home.

THE IMPORTANCE OF INTENTION

According to the dictionary, *intention* is a determination to act in a certain way or to reach a particular goal. Every move you make in martial arts must be done with an attitude of purpose. Without intention, you are already defeated!

Sensei Tabuchi says that when breaking a brick with your hand, you must not focus on the top; otherwise, as soon as you feel its resistance you will stop. Not only will you not break the brick, but you will more than likely hurt your hand. You must aim your energy through the entire stack some 6 inches below the last brick, so that it does not stop until you reach that spot. When you set your intention *beyond* the brick, you have already broken it. The same is true for mental blocks.

When negotiating, your intention is equally driven by focus. You must decide that you want to buy or sell some object and then focus on the entire process straight through to the end. One of the biggest challenges real estate agents have is with homeowners who aren't quite sure they want to sell. Even though they need to sell for financial or other reasons, they are just too emotionally attached to a home in which children grew up and where there are many fond memories. Smart agents will try to move them out of the past, into the present, and on to the future by painting a picture of how they could enjoy the money from the sale or how they could be closer to their grandchildren by moving.

Most sellers of large-ticket items that have sentimental value go through a period of mourning before they can part with the items. Give them permission to think about all the memories one more time, and then begin to reframe their thoughts to why they need to sell and how the transaction might contribute to a brighter future.

Buyers also go through a period of hesitation during which their intentions are unclear. You might know you need a new car but really can't make up your mind. The old one is unreliable and the cost of repair would be very high, yet it has been faithful for eight years. Allow yourself to let the old car go, and then begin to picture yourself driving a new one. Actually go into a dealership and have the salespeople take pictures of you sitting behind the wheel of their cars. Have fun with this, and you'll discover that in the process, your intention will become much clearer.

Just know that you may not be aware of your own intent. Believe it or not, sometimes your real intention might be to fail. Watch the words you say or think when a negotiating opportunity arises. If you hear yourself using a phrase such as "I'll try," "I'll do the best I can," or "I'll see if it works," then you are declaring failure before you have even begun. You are simply playing to lose.

You're just providing the excuse up front and giving yourself a way out for when you do lose. As the wise sage Yoda, from the *Star Wars* movies, used to say, "There is no try." People who really intend to win say what they *will* do, not what they will *try to* do. Football coaches, in the locker room before a game, do not tell their squad, "I want you to try to win today." They just tell them to win.

Martial artists expect to win by using phrases such as "When I win . . . ," "After I defeat my opponent . . . ," and "When victory is mine . . ." If you enter a negotiation and you want to win, then you must expect to win. When negotiating the purchase of some item, say to yourself, "After I have successfully concluded our negotiations . . ." or "Once I own this, I will . . ." When bargaining on the sale of some possession, you can say, "After I've made a solid profit off of this, I'll go out and buy . . ."

Once you decide to move forward, you must fully engage your intention. Just as you would never hit a brick simply to test it out, you should never be tentative about negotiating. Focus all your energies on the goal of winning, not on why you can't.

Once you decide that you want to negotiate on some item, shoot for the best deal possible. When you are dealing with a capable opponent, do not worry about the fairness of the deal. If the opponent should have been more prepared, more alert, more focused, or better trained and the person isn't, that is *not* your problem. Remember, if the other party agrees to your deal, everyone's happy.

WHITE BELT TEST

Before you can move up the ranks in martial arts, you must be tested to prove that you have learned the skills taught at this level. In tae kwon do, Sensei Tabuchi tests all white belts to make sure they can recite the Martial Arts Code, can set a firm stance, and know the basics of punching and blocking.

A white belt in negotiating must know the basics as well. Here's a test to determine what you know before moving on.

1. Name three similarities between martial arts and negotiating.
2. In nonnegotiating cultures, what items do people commonly negotiate?

3. What items do Asians, Hispanics, and Middle Easterners commonly negotiate?
4. How would you define *negotiating*?
5. Complete the following: "Negotiating is not _____."
6. Who tend to be better negotiators, men or women? Why?
7. Name two traits many women share that give them a negotiating advantage.
8. How would your life be different if you were a better negotiator?
9. Why do people in industrialized countries tend to negotiate less than those in other countries?
10. What does the black belt stand for?
11. Who are the best negotiators in the world? Why?
12. How do martial artists overcome fear?
13. Why do most people fear negotiations?
14. Why is the fear of negotiations totally unfounded?
15. What's another reason people are often reluctant to negotiate?
16. Why are most businesses willing to give some customers a discount?
17. How do many experienced negotiators calm their nerves when starting a bargaining session?
18. Name one fear you have about negotiating.
19. Why is fear a positive force when negotiating?
20. Why is win-win a flawed philosophy?

Do not move to Chapter 4 until you have answered the preceding questions and feel comfortable with your answers and have completed the following exercise.

The Graduation Test

Once new martial artists have shown their knowledge, they must then demonstrate basic skills. You can do this in negotiating by putting all the receipts and charge slips for everything you buy for two weeks into a shoe box. At the end of the two weeks, go through them and ask yourself, "Did I miss an opportunity to negotiate?"

Add up all the receipts for expenses that you could have negotiated, multiply the total by 15 percent (.15), and then multiply that amount by 26. This two-week sample shows how much you could accumulate in a year if you had saved 15 percent on those purchases by bargaining for an entire year.

Are you ready to start saving? Read on.

PART II

Yellow Belt

The seed sees the sunlight and begins to grow.
At this stage, students learn to develop strengths they didn't know they had.
New knowledge is opening up their minds and
preparing them to gain and use power.

Upon passing the white belt test, students are awarded their first colored belt which differentiates them from the raw beginners. In the Chapter 4—"Learning the Rules of Power"—yellow belts will come to understand the hidden rules of power that the average person is unaware of. Negotiators will discover their own rules for gaining the upper hand, like how to use leverage, momentum, power and focus.

The next part of martial arts training is learning how to observe fellow students and spy on opponents as they train to gain a sense of their own strengths and weaknesses. They know that in the next stage, they will actually have to spar, and they had better find out valuable information ahead of time about those they will be sparring with. In Chapter 5—"Spying on Your Opponent"—negotiators will discover that there are many ways to ascertain what an opponent is up to before sitting down at the bargaining table.

In Chapter 6—"Identify Vital Striking Points"—fighters will use all the information they have learned so far to increase their accuracy and identify the vulnerable areas on an opponent so they know where to concentrate their energy. This will earn them big points when they begin actually sparring when they receive their green belt. They are also shown how to focus their mind and breathe in a way that supports concentration. Similarly, negotiators will learn how to probe for what the other party really wants—and will give something up to get. That is how one makes sure his needs are met in a negotiation. People don't have to enter a bargaining session totally in the dark if they follow the principles in this chapter.

4

Learning the Rules of Power

*You can learn to find and generate power from sources
you would never have expected.*
SENSEI TABUCHI

In martial arts there are basic rules about how to develop and use power, and black belts know those rules. Masters live and breathe the rules, all of which are based on scientific principles.

The technical definition of *power* is "mass multiplied by velocity squared." This means that you can generate the same power if you have less mass by hitting faster. The best martial artist at this skill was Bruce Lee, who, at 5 feet, 7 inches tall and just 140 pounds, was no heavyweight, yet he was able to defeat much larger opponents because he was so fast and so focused.

During negotiations, power is generated through a number of techniques including blocking, using leverage, and building momentum. The following are the most common ways to develop power during the bargaining process.

Blocking

Although this may seem counterintuitive, blocking is actually one of the most powerful moves in martial arts because if you learn to block effectively, you cannot be hit. Throughout a confrontation, your opponent is expending his or her energy, yet you are using little of yours. It is said that if you learn to block expertly, you would never have to learn to punch or kick; the fight would end when your opponent realized it was futile to try to hit you or when he or she simply wore out.

In negotiating, blocking means learning to anticipate your opponent's moves before he or she can make them, and you prepare a countermove to offset them. You have to think about all the proposals or objections that could be offered and how you might respond to them. Essentially, this means putting yourself in the other person's place, asking yourself "what if" questions.

You might want to go to a movie opening with your boyfriend. Ask yourself, "What if he resists because it's a chick flick?" You could point out that there are always attractive women in chick flicks, and that should keep him happy.

If you make a request without being prepared for an objection, you leave yourself wide open without a defense or an answer. In fact, the most powerful way to deal with an objection is to answer it *before* it arises. Blocking objections in this way gives you power and increased confidence.

Using Leverage

Leverage is the ability to multiply force using a lever on a fulcrum. It enables you to use a small amount of force to gain a large amount of movement; it allows a 90-pound woman to throw a 300-pound man with ease. By shifting their footwork just slightly, martial artists can change the leverage and alter the outcome of the match. The art of judo, in fact, is based totally on leverage. In this case, the lever is your opponent's body, while the fulcrum is your hip, knee, or another part of your body.

In negotiating, leverage has many uses. Often, it is employed when a lot of people want something that is in short supply. For example, when the Honda Accord was first imported into America from Japan in 1976, it had a reputation for reliability and fuel economy just when the supply of gasoline became short. Consequently, there was a waiting list six months long to get one. The price rapidly rose until some dealers were able to get nearly twice the original retail price. That's leverage in action.

Judo masters recognize that when someone pushes another person, there is a natural tendency to push back. One of the basic rules of the art is that instead of reacting normally, practitioners should simply step back or step to the side and redirect the opponent's energy wherever they wish. Similarly, when an opponent tries to punch them, judo experts will use the person's own energy to throw him or her to the ground.

When someone puts pressure on you in negotiating, that is the perfect time to use leverage: Take the pressure that the other party is placing on you, recognize that it is making the person unstable, and use this knowledge to shift the leverage in your favor. A common example of this occurs all the time in time-share sales. I deliberately set our appointment for our sales presentation early in the morning in case I need the end of the day to return to finish the deal. This gives me the leverage of time. When salespeople tell me that "this offer is good only today," they don't seem to realize they are basically positioning themselves at the edge of a cliff. I can push them off by simply walking away. If I'm truly interested in buying a unit, I will come back late in the afternoon. I am in a position to make a better deal because I called their bluff—when the day is almost over and they are really under pressure to make the sale.

At one point in negotiations, one person always appears to have more leverage than another. However, the advantage can be fleeting, and you have to be prepared to seize it. For instance, a home seller may have the leverage if there are three buyers who all want to purchase her home. However, while the greedy seller is trying to decide which offer is better, one buyer might find a house that is more suitable and another could be transferred out of town. By that time, the leverage quickly shifts to the lone remaining purchaser. If this is you, the trick is to act quickly while the advantage is available to you before another buyer appears on the scene to compete with you and cause you to lose the advantage. With no other buyers in sight, you could now ask for that hot tub you had been eyeing or withdraw your current offer and submit a new one at a lower price.

Another way to gain leverage is to increase your buying power. You can buy in bulk by getting friends and relatives to purchase at the same time. Many retailers offer bulk sale discounts to reward those who purchase larger quantities, if they don't, ask how much you'd have to buy to get a deal. New-home builders have reported that several families from negotiating cultures will often buy several homes at the same time and reap a substantial savings. My wife and I bought our cars at the same time from the same dealer and got a tremendous deal because we were buying two cars instead of just one.

When you are going to make a major purchase, call or e-mail your friends and family to determine whether any of them have the same need. You might negotiate a bit more of the savings for yourself for having gone to the trouble of putting the buying group together.

Building Momentum

Momentum is defined as "mass in motion." Mathematically, it is defined as mass times velocity. In martial arts in general and judo in particular, momentum is crucial. In judo, everything is done using your opponents' momentum against them. As mentioned earlier, a judo master redirects a punch away from its target and uses that energy to throw the person to the ground.

In negotiating, the motion of the parties moving toward or away from agreement can be used by sharp negotiators to help them win. If you see an agreement gaining momentum, you can run with the forward energy to add to your gains. Let's say the other party obviously wants to close the deal; you might ask for a few more concessions at the last moment to capitalize on the person's desire to get it over with.

The momentum moving away from an agreement can be just as beneficial in creating a big win, even though victory seems far from likely at that point. My real estate partner, Stuart, and I once sat down with a seller who was putting up all kinds of objections to our offers. Whatever positive momentum we started with was rapidly slipping away. Suddenly, Stuart jumped up, saying, "This is ridiculous. We've made a very generous offer and they seem to think they can do better. I'm outta here!" Then he stomped out, leaving a very stunned seller, along with his agent and me, all staring at each other. Just then I noticed that Stuart had left a slip of paper in my lap suggesting that I wait thirty seconds, then offer just $500 more than our original price. I apologized for my partner's actions and then did exactly as his note suggested.

Stuart's abrupt departure had taken the somewhat negative tone of the seller and made the atmosphere even more dark and depressing—a strange thing to do, since the momentum was decidedly in the opposite direction of closing the deal. Yet we turned it around because my offer to raise the price only slightly suddenly seemed like a gracious gesture, like a brilliant ray of sunshine, and so the seller eagerly accepted it. In this way, we used the momentum going against us to flip a potential loss into a big win.

Testing the Wind

When you are sparring outdoors, the direction of the wind can influence the outcome of the contest. If you are facing the wind, dust and debris can blow into your eyes, so naturally you want the wind at your back. In negotiations, you don't need to literally test the wind, but you can assess the conditions in which the game is taking place. This enables you to determine in which direction the momentum is heading so you can plan your next move or, better, your next three moves.

You must constantly test the direction of the market before you make an offer to buy or put an item up for sale. Is it a buyers' or sellers' market? Is there competition? Are prices going up or down? Is there increasing or decreasing demand for your product? Are interest rates rising or falling? Is this the first or last day of a sale?

In January, clothing retailers begin to advertise their spring fashions, and discounts are rare because it's a sellers' market. However, as summer ends and winter clothes begin to make their appearance, sales on spring fashions are increasingly common. There's no room on the shelves for both seasons' clothes, so this is the perfect time to shop for next April's wardrobe. Another factor that can drive the price down is several manufacturers carrying similar styles at the same time. Making a conscious choice about when to shop for what you want based on the market's need to sell can save you a lot of money.

The basic principle here is that you should always flow with the wind, not against it. Sell when demand and prices are high, and buy when demand and prices are low, but don't be greedy. There's an ancient Chinese proverb that says, "Only a fool believes he knows when the wind will change." In other words, don't try to get the absolute highest or lowest price, because you could get burned. Like experienced negotiators, savvy investors in the stock market know to take a couple of modest profits and move on, rather than waiting for one big score. Bars and saloons are littered with people who missed their one big score.

Flowing with the Power, Not Against It

It's a common misconception that you can win over another person's heart and mind through an argument, but you can't. Statistics show that people choose basic beliefs in significant areas like politics and religion very early in life, and most of them die holding those same beliefs. Do you really expect to change a person's core ideology during a brief negotiation? It is far more effective to understand what people want and then appear to give it to them. One of the first lessons that beginning martial artists learn is never to meet power with power because the only result will likely be a broken bone. One of the favorite techniques that Sensei Tabuchi uses to teach students this lesson is called *bone blocking*. If you think you can overpower a martial arts master by hitting him with everything you've got, he will block your move with a sharp elbow. This just ends up hurting you instead of him.

In negotiating, an argumentative position is an attack position, which only makes your opponent more defensive. She could easily move away from giving you what you want, instead of moving toward you. Even people on a college debate team, a clear situation in which the stated purpose is to score points, realize that they could ultimately lose the match by overworking a point. Continuing their assault will only back the other team into a corner, and then all they want to do is fight back. Being argumentative and disagreeable when making a deal could cause the other person to resent you and make major parts of the negotiation more difficult. Which is more important, winning an argument or getting the deal you want?

This is where women tend to have an advantage. The language women use is usually less argumentative and more concerned with feelings than that of men. As a result, they are less likely to argue than their male counterparts.

If your opponent makes a statement that you absolutely disagree with, or even that you find insulting, resist the natural temptation to snap back with an aggressive response that can only lead to a quarrel. An effective technique is *counting to ten* before you say anything. It's an old one, but it does indeed work because it gives you time to calm down and respond more rationally than emotionally.

I find that if I listen and ask questions, my opponent's resistance softens, and the person will begin to work with me rather than against me. It's all about flowing with power rather than against it. To avoid offering a response that could lead to an argument and to give you time to think, you can simply ask one of these questions:

- Can you tell me why you say that?
- Can you tell me why you feel that way?
- Can you tell me why you need us to structure the deal like that?

Any kind of "Can you tell me . . . " question not only gives you time to cool off while the other party is constructing an answer, thus avoiding an awkward silence, it also buys you goodwill because it suggests that you are genuinely interested in the other party's opinion. And there's always the chance that the person's answer could entirely change the course of the conversation. What you previously thought was a totally unreasonable request on the other person's part may now make perfect sense to you, and maybe you can find some way to work with the response. Once the person has explained his or her position, you have the opportunity to educate the person about why you cannot meet the demands precisely the way he or she wants. Although you cannot argue other people into changing their minds, you can certainly educate them into working with a different perspective—yours. Asking questions can help you understand what people want and appear to give it to them.

If you want to see an example of people who have turned questioning into an art, just watch children trying to talk their parents into buying them the latest video game. Children work hard at bargaining because it's about the only power they have. No matter what fabulous answer you have when a child asks, "Will you buy me that game?" your logic is crushed by the weight of the child's next question, "Why?" All parents learn, sooner or later, that getting into a power struggle with children is a losing proposition. If you give in after a half hour of constant questioning, the children have just witnessed the strength of their power and they become hungry for more. If you succeed in enforcing your will upon them, they will attribute this to your power as an adult and will only long for the day when they can wield that kind of power themselves. Instead of increasing your show of power when you meet resistance from your children, just ask a "Can you tell me . . . ?" question and then watch as the struggle for power vanishes. Children relish telling adults their reasons for wanting what they want, and this gives you a chance to give them a choice between two better alternatives, such as a book or educational game. This shows them the strength of educating rather than arguing.

If someone *insists* on arguing with you, simply use the *feel, felt, found* technique. For example, if you are a salesperson in a computer store and a buyer says, "I know I can get a better deal online," you simply reply, "I know how you feel. In fact, I've felt the same way myself. What I've found, though, is that the advantage of saving a few dollars online can be easily wiped out by the lack of technical support or the cost of shipping the item back for repair and then the long wait until it's fixed. We're right here to take care of you. You don't have to send an expensive electronic device to some post office box in India." You can see why it's hard to argue with really good logic.

Using Guile

You use guile when you are being cunning by concealing your intentions and by being unpredictable. Hiding your motives is not lying; it's just not being obvious, which gives away your true position.

In a martial arts tournament, cagey fighters sometimes hang their heads and pretend to breathe hard as if they are exhausted. Suddenly, they spring to life, catching their opponent off guard.

You can do the same in negotiations. One day on vacation in Jamaica, I wanted to find out what the down-and-dirty price would be for a T-shirt, especially since I would be buying quite a few of them as souvenirs for friends. The best deal I could find was at a shop that was selling three shirts for $15. Now, $5 each is not too bad a deal, but this was an opportunity to practice my bargaining skills in a country that is world famous for negotiating. Without disclosing how many I really wanted, I started by asking the price of six shirts. The lady behind the counter smiled and said, "Four dollars and fifty cents each." I went up to nine shirts and received another predictable discount. Finally she looked at me with a gleam in her eye and said, "Mister, how many do you really want to buy?" Having been found out, I told her a dozen, and we finally settled on $3.50 apiece.

The second use of guile is being unpredictable. In a martial arts tournament, this is essential to your very survival. Jabbing is only a half-punch or kick toward an area; it brings your opponent's guard down so you can follow up with a full punch or kick to a different part of the body that scores points. It can be very effective, but against an experienced fighter, if you *always* jab before you punch, you may as well hang a sign around your neck saying, "Right after this jab I'm going to punch, so get ready to block me and then counter with whatever you want because I'm now going to be vulnerable to it." Guile requires mixing jabs with punches and kicks to different parts of the body so your opponent cannot discern any kind of predictable pattern. In other words, guile means not giving yourself away.

In negotiating, you can be unpredictable in many ways. For example, try offering a little more than a seller is asking. Why on earth would you do that?

To throw the seller off balance, and while the person is reeling with surprise, you might ask him or her to pay the shipping costs or the sales tax, which more than makes up for the price you offered.

Women, in particular, can use unpredictability to their advantage. One way is to let men think you won't be aggressive in a negotiation. It's not hard to do, since it so neatly fits the stereotype that many men already believe about women. At the appropriate time, turn into a predator and press your case. I saw one woman allow her male counterpart to dictate everything he wanted. Once his cards were clearly face up on the table, she said, "Thanks for sharing this information. Now let me tell you what I'm prepared to do, and if you don't like my proposal, I must inform you that I have three other companies ready to accept the same deal. Although I personally like you, this deal is dead the minute I walk out the door." Upon hearing this, the male negotiator was so taken aback by her unexpected aggressiveness that he just signed her contract without even a whimper of protest. Unpredictability will throw your opponents off balance, and while they're in that state, you can take the upper hand.

Practicing guile does not mean you are being unethical. It is simply the same as not putting all your cards on the table until the appropriate time in a game of poker. Although honesty is important in building a trusting relationship, you still might want to conceal your intentions. Saying less than you need to say is always a wise policy.

Disguising Your Weaknesses

All martial artists have weaknesses. Their punches may lack power or their kicks may be extended a bit too long, leaving them especially vulnerable. Weaknesses can't be helped; this doesn't mean, however, that you have to broadcast them to your opponent.

Sensei Tabuchi relates the story of a fighter who had a foot injury and could kick only from the left side. However, he was able to disguise the kicks from his one good leg so well that it was almost as if he had two good legs. Opponents never knew if they were going to see a hook kick, round kick, front kick, or side kick. As a result, he became a champion by maximizing his strengths (using the good leg for the real work) and concealing his weaknesses (only jabbing with the weak leg).

Negotiators must also find ways to compensate for their weaknesses. Whatever bargaining situation we are faced with, we will always be vulnerable to some kind of chink in our armor. We may have a limited budget, be caught in a time crunch, or have little flexibility to change the options. But we don't have to broadcast any of this. If you are up against a fast-approaching deadline, for instance, act as if you have all the time in the world. If your bank account has less money than your kid's piggy bank, find ways to gain leverage by making nonmonetary concessions.

Sometimes you must expose your flaws, yet even this can be turned to your favor. A classic example is when you are applying for a job and an interviewer says, "Describe one of your weaknesses and how it impacts your performance." This could be a land mine if you are not prepared with an honest-sounding, insightful answer. Whenever I am faced with this situation I tell interviewers that I am a bit of a workaholic (I was using guile because I am more than just a *bit* of a workaholic) and that sometimes I expect the people I supervise to work just as hard. Although some may consider workaholism to be a disease, employers love to hire such people for obvious reasons, so I presented as a flaw something I knew they would actually find attractive.

Job counselors will tell you that this classic question about describing your weaknesses is the perfect opportunity to discuss how you turned them into strengths. Talk about the lessons you learned from making mistakes. This demonstrates that you used a strike against you and turned it into a point in your favor. It also shows that you know how to learn from your mistakes.

Finding Your Power

Every win is achieved from a position of power. The beauty of martial arts is that you can learn to find and generate power from sources you would never have expected. Another perk is that everyone can compete. Young and old, tall and short, thin and heavy, it doesn't matter. Steady practitioners will always find a strength regardless of their body type or relative fitness.

Women especially tend to underestimate their power because they are less strong in the upper body than men. However, in martial arts they can use the strength in their lower body to be competitive by employing kicks more than punches. Because their center of gravity is lower, their power is usually found between their hips and their toes. Most women in martial arts will just feint with their hands as a setup for kicks. Also, their flexibility is greater, giving them an advantage in doing spins and twisting moves.

Men tend to be more dominant in upper-body strength, so they usually excel at punches and arm blocks. A man is actually challenged when sparring with a woman who is a good kicker because her legs are longer than his arms; she can usually reach him before he can contact her.

You have much more bargaining power than you think. Don't forget that other parties are negotiating for a reason. If they could just take what they wanted, they probably would. Instead, they have to find a way to convince you to agree to their deal. There is power in that alone. Also, there must be something in it for them to feel like winners. Your job is to find out what it is and use it to win yourself. You might be weak in some way, but do not assume that your opponent recognizes what that weakness is. It may seem glaringly apparent to you, but it's rarely that obvious to the other side.

At first glance, for example, it may appear that children have little power. However, watch children go after what they set their hearts on in a toy store and you witness how they get what they want. Without any money of their own, they use the power of persistence to let their parents know over and over again that they want, for example, the latest Barbie doll. If the parents say no, the kids start whining, "I want Barbie, I want Barbie." If that doesn't have the desired effect, the children will start crying hysterically, but every once in a while you'll clearly hear them say "Barbie." More often than not, a child who uses this tactic will walk out of the store with the doll just because she was persistent. Statistics show that children will ask for something twenty-nine times before giving up. How many parents can outlast that onslaught?

Focusing Your Power

The reason that focus gives you power is that it concentrates your strength in one place to the greatest effect. A punch, in fact, has no power unless it is concentrated on a small area. By directing all my energy into just the edge of my palm and focusing that power onto the center of a stack of concrete slabs, I can break a total of eight inches of concrete. If I used all the meat of my hand, I wouldn't be able to do it and would probably break my wrist.

In negotiating, focus is just as crucial to your success. Try not to be distracted by side issues that might come up or by necessary pleasantries. You must learn to selectively focus from one issue to the next while keeping the big picture in mind. The whole point of negotiating is to meet all of your needs and most of your wants, so always keep your eye on the prize. You must not leave until all your needs are met and as many of your wants as possible have been obtained. I know people who go into their doctor's office with a list of questions, but leave with only one of them answered. With busy doctors, you are always negotiating for more time. Before they've even entered the room, they have one foot out the door to see their next patient. You have to keep that list of questions in the front of your mind and not let the doctor go until they are answered.

Bargaining with More Powerful Opponents

It's not unusual in a tournament to find yourself competing against someone who has more skill, power, and experience than you. No matter what you do, the opponent just seems to be one step ahead. No matter how fast you are, the other person always seems to get there first. When you find yourself in this situation, all you can do is the best you can to score a few points. Your real gain is experience for the future.

In negotiating, you may be bargaining with your boss or your spouse. In either case, you must select a few key issues you want to win, and the rest you know you will have to concede. In this situation, focus is absolutely critical. Again, having a clear list of needs and wants will come in handy in this situation.

Martial artists are taught to immediately go into a defensive posture when facing stronger opponents. Although you may not win the tournament, you don't want to be defeated right away. You want to stall for time to find an opening or a weakness. To teach this skill, Sensei Tabuchi would stick a balloon on a student and his or her only goal was to protect it while another student would try to pop it with kicks or punches. The teacher might attach it to the chest, the left arm, or the right leg so the student learns to protect different parts of the body.

Similarly, when they are against someone in a stronger position, negotiators must protect their own positions first and then try to gain as much ground as possible. For instance, in a home sellers' market where there are few properties available and many buyers, it's a given that you are going to pay at or above the asking price. However, the buyer can still ask for inspections, a specific closing date, a home warranty, for the seller to carry back a second loan, and more.

Martial artists know to fall back on their fundamentals when facing a stronger opponent. There are always a few techniques you are really good at, and you can simply use those. This is not the time to get fancy. However, you can still win using just a few basics. Sensei Tabuchi relates a story about a grand champion who won tournaments using only two techniques that everyone knew he was limited to, but he was so good with them that he still won anyway.

Negotiators must also rely on their fundamentals. One of the most powerful tools when dealing with a much stronger opponent is to conduct as much research as you possibly can in advance. That is the subject of Chapter 5.

5

Spying on Your Opponent

No matter how much strength, weaponry, and capability the enemy has,
if you can find the one weak point that will bring him to his knees,
he can be defeated.

SUN-TZU

Although every chapter in this book can help you become a superb negotiator, this one on spying is probably the most crucial. The power of this technique is attested by Sun-tzu (544–496 BC), who was a general and the author of *The Art of War,* an immensely influential ancient Chinese book on military strategy. The general said that most battles are over before they begin if one side knows it's enemy's weak points. "Advance knowledge cannot be gained from ghosts and spirits, inferred from phenomena, or projected from the measures of Heaven, but must be gained from men for it is the knowledge of the enemy's true situation." Of course, he also stressed the importance of possessing the right character traits if you are going to use subterfuge. "Unless someone has the wisdom of a Sage, he cannot use spies; unless he is benevolent and righteous, he cannot employ spies; unless he is subtle and perspicacious, he cannot perceive the substance in intelligence reports. It is subtle, subtle! There are no areas in which one does not employ spies."

No matter how much strength, weaponry, and capability enemies have, if you can find the one weak point that will bring them to their knees, then they can be defeated—period. No amount of strength can cover a core weakness.

Martial artists know that there are vulnerable areas in all bodies, and they can turn even the fiercest warriors into whimpering, helpless children if they strike them there. Clearly, being able to identify places of weakness allows them to bring their opponents down, even if the opponents are twice their size. Information that helps identify weak spots turns out to be more powerful than superior physique or advanced weapons.

This is why, before any contest, martial artists will learn everything they can about their opponents by finding opportunities to watch them train and spar. Sensei Tabuchi suggests that before you climb into the ring with people, watch videotapes of them fighting. You can learn what style they practice, whether they are left- or right-handed, and any weaknesses they might exhibit.

Prior to a negotiation, you can also search out many sources of information to give yourself an edge. Let's say you have a coworker who's been going around the office trying to sell two tickets to a Rolling Stones concert, and this person has a reputation for always getting the better end of a deal. Before he approaches you, do a little innocent spying. Find out how much he tried to get for the tickets from your other coworkers. What was the best offer? Go on the Internet and find out if the concert is sold out, which would make these premium tickets and worth more than their face value. Is the concert coming up soon or is it months away? If it's months away, he's not under much pressure to give you a bargain price. Asking appropriate questions at the outset will give you the leverage to present an initial offer that is as low as possible. If you didn't know this, you might just give the seller his asking price, but instead you found out everything you needed to know by asking others before he approached you. If you had asked him for the information, he might not have given you an honest answer. After all, he has his own interests to protect.

Much of the information you need in order to gain an edge in negotiations is readily available from sources such as public records, product catalogs, the Internet, and other people. Mostly, common sense will tell you where to search. Negotiations come in many forms, and being armed with information will always work in your favor. For example, before discussing with your son whether he can join the football team, talk to other parents about what the risks are and ask whether it has caused their kids' grades to suffer. If you are applying for a job, you can easily find out what salary workers in similar positions are receiving by checking with job placement agencies. Before putting your kids in day care, check out the costs, quality of the facility, and training the staff receives, and then research what the competition is like in the area. Never walk into a negotiation without doing your research.

Before buying my most recent car from the dealer, I did research online and found out what he had paid for the vehicle and the cost of all the options. Since I was leasing it, I knew that the dealer did not have a lot of flexibility on the price but he could deal with me on the terms and conditions. I used that to my advantage to effectively lower the price by getting him to throw in 25,000 extra miles over five years. It cost him nearly nothing but saved me $6,250 in penalties. Not bad for ten minutes' research on the Internet.

Remember, people who are buying or selling something are doing so because they are trying to solve a problem. A bit of healthy spying will tell you what that problem is and how you can use that information to your advantage. If their need is critical, if the time is short, or if their discomfort level is high, that person has a strong motivation to make a deal, and you can leverage that to push for terms that work in your favor. The key is to find out why they are selling or buying, which means asking questions. Start by digging for clues. If you can help them solve their problems, they are more likely to give you what you want.

THE INTERVIEW AS A SPYING TECHNIQUE

Sometimes you'll find that the best source of information comes right from the horse's mouth. Simply by asking direct questions in a nonthreatening manner, you can quickly discern whether or not this is the right person to be talking to.

Buying Products

You will undoubtedly need to find the answers to some of these questions through research before you talk to the seller. Others, you can ask the seller directly.

- What similar products are available? (research)
- What is the cost of similar products? (research)
- How many other people are interested? (research)
- Why are you selling this product?
- How long have you been in business?

- How much do you expect to obtain for your product?
- What's unique or special about your product?
- How did you determine your price?
- What options are available?
- What is your deadline for selling?
- Does this ever go on sale? If so, when?

Selling Products

When selling products, you should answer some of these questions in advance of talking to the buyer (research), and others you can ask the buyer directly.

- How large is the pool of potential buyers? (research)
- Is there an optimum time to be selling this product? (research)
- Why are you considering purchasing this product at this time?
- Have you purchased one of these before?
- What attributes are most important to you?
- Are you considering a similar product? What?
- What will you primarily be using the product for?
- Will you be paying cash or financing? (on major purchases)
- Do you have a deadline for buying?
- If you don't buy this, what would you use the money for?

Buying Services

The challenge with buying medical, legal, accounting, and other services is that they are intangible and unique to the provider. The biggest concern is usually not how cheaply you can obtain the service but that it be done right.

- What services are customarily provided? (research)
- What differentiates good service from great service? (research)
- What is an average price for this service? (research)
- What are your qualifications for providing this service?
- How long have you been doing this kind of work?

- Who's your main competitor?
- How are you different from that competitor?
- Do you have some references I could contact?
- Do you guarantee your services?
- Do you offer a discount for advance payment?

Selling Services

The challenge with selling services is that in the best-case scenario, you end up with a client who appreciates you and what you have to offer. If it's going to be a long-term relationship, it really helps if you personally like the client. These questions will help you sort out what the client's expectations are and what he or she is bringing to the table.

- What services are customarily provided by competitors? (research)
- What differentiates good service from great service? (research)
- What do similar providers charge for this service? (research)
- Why are you seeking my help?
- How did you happen to choose me?
- Have you ever used a service like mine before?
- If so, what was your experience?
- Exactly what would you expect from someone like me?
- How would you define a successful relationship between us?
- If I meet your needs, would you be willing to refer others?

Partnering

Joining together with one or more people to go into business is one of the most important decisions anyone can make. To make sure your needs are met, consider the following questions:

- What is the other person's background? (research)
- What kind of intellectual and financial resources does the person have? (research)
- What is the other person's track record in this kind of business? (research)

- Why do I want to go into partnership with this person?
- What does this person bring to the table that I do not have?
- Are we emotionally compatible?
- Would I enjoy spending time with this person away from work?
- What is my definition of success?
- What is the other person's definition of success?
- Will we both agree to put our goals in writing?
- How will we break a deadlock?

THE VALUE OF ASKING GOOD QUESTIONS

Answering the preceding questions should give you the edge you need to figure out whether to buy, sell, partner, and so on. They are just the tip of the iceberg, though; feel free to add your own, depending on the situation. As every savvy newspaper reporter knows, the quality of the questions you ask determines the quality of the answers you receive. Therefore, they must be concise and elicit the information you seek. Asking the wrong questions, or asking the right ones in the wrong way, or making general inquiries that provide you with a lot of details you don't need, is a waste of time. When done right, interviewing is an incredibly powerful way to obtain the information you need and want. Just make sure that the other person stops, listens to what you are saying, comes up with a real answer, and responds. Being a smart interviewer immediately puts you in control. Remember: "The quality of the information determines the quality of the negotiation."

Be careful how you phrase your questions because they can be unknowingly offensive. Women tend to be much more adept at asking questions without creating offense. Perhaps it's because they are instinctively able to put themselves in the other person's shoes and know what would and wouldn't be taken as a slight. They also seem more apt to ask questions in the first place, instead of marching right in with an offer. This is probably because they invested less of their egos in the situation. Many men seem to feel that asking questions implies that they aren't very smart, so they are reluctant to say anything that would indicate they don't have all the answers. Perhaps this is why some men drive around lost for hours before asking for directions.

One thing you have working in your favor is that many people actually like answering questions because it makes them feel important to be the knowledge holder, even if the only thing they know is the directions to Wal-Mart. Another factor is that asking a question implies that you are asking for help, and people like to be helpful. On more than one occasion I have been given far more information than people ever intended because they wanted to help me and their inhibitions were relaxed as a result of my questions.

Unfortunately, the most common tack that most people take when entering a negotiation is to be focused on "What's in it for me?" It's just human nature to be primarily concerned about our own welfare. We forget that if we want other people to be motivated to do something for us, we must make sure they first see what's in it for them. Smart spies are extremely interested in learning what their opponents expect to get out of this deal, because this information will help them anticipate their next move, understand and work with the person's resistance, and develop leverage by giving up something important to the opponent yet insignificant to themselves. One small sacrifice made at the right time can yield an extraordinary return. There is great benefit in being less self-absorbed and more other-oriented.

Previously, we looked at specific questions for specific situations. Now we want to pay attention to two important types of questions you will use in a negotiation and the types of answers they elicit.

Open Questions

These usually begin with the words *who, what, who, where, why,* or *how,* and they cannot usually be answered with a yes or a no or with a number. They are more likely to elicit truthful information because they require more thought than closed questions. They also let you see more incongruence between your opponent's body language and what the person is saying, as opposed to asking questions that require only short answers.

Here are some examples of open questions:

- *Who* has the authority to give me a discount?
- *What* kind of discount did you have in mind?
- *When* did you plan on buying?
- *Where* is our biggest area of disagreement?
- *Why* do you want this product or service?
- *How* do you plan on using it?

Closed Questions

These elicit information, confirm your understanding of the situation or deal, or seek commitment. Closed questions can generally be answered only with a yes or a no or with a number.

Here are some examples of closed questions:

- *Do* you like this product?
- *If* I guaranteed immediate delivery, would you buy today?
- *Can* you think of a reason not to do this?
- *Would* you like to take this with you?
- *Should* I wrap this for you?

SOURCES OF INFORMATION

Spies will use any avenue available to gather data. You never know where you'll find the answers you need; they could be as close as the Internet or the phone book.

The best spies know how and where to get information on their opponents without even approaching them, something you shouldn't do because it could tip them off to the fact that you are interested. Here are some common sources of valuable data:

- If you're looking to buy a piece of property, county records are available that will tell you who owns a particular piece of property, how long they have owned it, what they originally paid for it, how much they owe on it, and more.
- If you're dating someone and considering entering into something as sacred and significant as marriage, you might want to know whether the person has been married before. Marriage and divorce information is a matter of public record.
- If you're considering the purchase of any piece of merchandise, just check the Internet to find out the rock-bottom price. But don't forget to add in the costs of shipping, warranties, and especially service. For many items, particularly those involving technology, it makes more sense to buy locally, where you have access to support. The Internet

price is still worth knowing, however, because it will give you leverage when negotiating.

- If you're thinking about going into partnership with someone, check the public records for bankruptcies and liens. If their financial abilities were deeply flawed in the past, why would they be any better now?
- If you're considering hiring a new employee, examine the public records to see whether the person has criminal convictions or is a registered sex offender. This advice could obviously be applied to partnerships as well.
- If you are a landlord, you might want to examine address histories in the public records, as well as unlawful detainer judgments, before renting to a new tenant. This could save you a lot of time and money in avoiding future evictions.

THE ART OF THE DEAL

In certain cases, you may need to obtain extensive information about your counterpart's business before you can even approach a subject of negotiation. I don't remember how it came about, but many years ago I got the crazy notion that I would like a discount on gasoline for my car. Over the years I had become friendly with my local dealer, Ahmed, and one day I simply asked him what the slowest day of the week for gas was. He thought for a moment and said, "Michael, that is a good question. Let me think. You know that Monday is very busy here with people filling-up after the weekend, Tuesday it slows down, and Wednesday is quiet. Then on Thursday and Friday people start filling up for the weekend and on Saturday and Sunday there is a line all the time. So Wednesday is our slowest day."

After pondering this deep question for a while, I just tested the waters by innocently asking if it would be better for his business if he sold more gas on Wednesdays. He smiled and said his overall gas costs would go down, but once it finally dawned on him where this conversation was headed, the smile turned to a look of concern. "Oh, Michael," he said, "we would have to sell much more gas than just your car for us to earn a discount from the distributor." I asked him about how much more he would need to sell, and he showed me on his calculator. The answer was 2,000 extra gallons, which he believed ended the discussion. I surprised him by responding, "So if I could help you sell two thousand more gallons a month on Wednesdays, what kind of a discount could I expect on that gas?" He hit a few more buttons on his trusty calculator and finally said, "I could give you three cents off a gallon." That amounted to a savings of about $.60 a fill-up. Clearly, this was not the deal of the century for me, but I kept playing the game anyway, and eventually we settled on a discount of $.10 a gallon. Saving this amount would hardly launch my lifestyle into the stratosphere, but the fun of being able to do what everyone said was impossible was worth the negotiation.

I did, however, end up earning my $.10 a gallon anyway simply by convincing all my friends in real estate to fill up at Ahmed's gas station on Wednesdays in return for the same low price. (No one uses more gas than real estate agents.) We regularly had forty people buying there, so we more than met our requirements for the discount.

Most people believe that there are products and services that are absolutely nonnegotiable. People who attend my negotiating seminars say that medical and dental care are two big ones, and they're right. They are among the most difficult areas to negotiate because we all need these services, there is a limited supply of trained professionals in these fields, and usually it doesn't even occur to us to pitch for a lower fee.

For instance, my wife wanted to buy those fancy invisible braces that cost about $5,000, so we let the dentist know we were interested but weren't willing to shell out $5,000 for them. Somehow, vacations seemed like a better way to spend our money. Two years later the dentist called and said that she could obtain brand-new braces for about half the former cost. Apparently, the patent on them was running out, and soon they would be widely available to other manufacturers. If we hadn't originally told the dentist that we would buy the braces if we could get them at a lower price, she would never have called us with the news. We immediately called for an appointment, and my wife is now wearing the miraculous braces that no one can see.

PLAN SO THAT THE NEGOTIATING ENVIRONMENT FAVORS YOU

All martial artists make themselves intimately acquainted with the location in which a contest is being held so that there aren't any surprises, distractions, or physical irritants to weaken their game. The ideal situation is always to be on your home turf because you are completely familiar with all the conditions there. Martial artists are accustomed to their own dojo and comfortable with every aspect of it, whereas they will feel uneasy in their opponent's. By negotiating to have the opponent come to you, you have the home field advantage every time.

Sometimes, however, we must meet opponents in their dojo. This is not the end of the world because often we can get a sense of it in advance simply by visiting as a prospective student at the same time of the day or night as the tournament. The visit enables us to determine such factors as lighting conditions, texture and thickness of the mat, overhead lighting, whether the sun is coming in from the windows (you always want the sun behind you so it is in your opponent's eyes), and anything else that might affect your performance. If we cannot perform even this step—the visit—then we are fighting blind, as they say, and must be ready for anything.

When you are entering a negotiation, you may not come to blows (at least I hope not), yet it's the same as a martial arts tournament in many ways, not the least of which is that you want to win. Whenever you possibly can, get your opponent to come to you. Inside your own office, you know what resources are available, such as the necessary forms, files, a showroom, a manager for consultation, and other forms of backup and reinforcement that could be of value.

On your opponent's home turf, you will always be a little more uncomfortable and off balance. In addition, almost everyone who is present at the meeting will be silently cheering for your opponent to win. Sports teams all know that when they're playing a game, their adrenaline goes up in a good way when the audience is applauding every time they score and booing their opponent. When the crowd is cheering *against* you, it can drain your energy and saddle you with a defeatist attitude in spite of your best efforts. The psychological effects of being on the other person's turf cannot be overestimated.

6

Identifying Vital Striking Points

Wants and needs can be strengths and weaknesses for both you and your opponent.

MICHAEL SOON LEE

Martial artists know they can take down the biggest opponent by hitting vital striking points, the places on the body that are the most vulnerable. Especially when defending yourself against dangerous people, such as thugs on the street, you should look for opportunities to hit attackers someplace that will stop them cold—such as the eyes, nose, throat, or groin. Self-defense classes stress these areas as the first point of attack.

In negotiations, your objective is to find the striking points on your opponent; this is where the person is most vulnerable. A vulnerable spot, in this case, isn't literally the jugular vein but the other person's needs. Answering "What do they want?" tells you what you can withhold as leverage to get what you want in return. This works the same way for both parties.

As mentioned earlier, before heading for the bargaining table, identify what your needs are. What is your objective? In martial arts, different situations can pose different objectives. For instance, when sparring in the dojo, the objective is to practice; in tournaments the objective is to win; in a street fight the objective is to survive. You can reach your own goals by anticipating your opponents' objectives because only by giving them something they want can you hope to get what you want. You can use the following five tactics to do so.

1. Clarify Your Own Wants and Needs

The point here is that before negotiating, you must first be clear about your own objectives. Start by making a list of your needs. These are the terms and conditions that must absolutely be met in order to make the deal acceptable to you. If you are looking for a mate, you might realize that you want him to have a certain level of education, have achieved a certain income level, own his own home, be considerate and kind, and have a sense of humor. If his income is in the high six figures, however, you might be willing to forgo the last two. If he lives with his mother, that could be a deal breaker. Figure out what you can't live without. The man, himself, is the need. It's quite possible that everything else is an add-on.

It's a good habit to keep your list of needs written down so in the heat of the discussion you don't lose track of them. Remember, the definition of a need is some part of the deal that you must absolutely have or it won't work for you. Guard your list of needs well because these are the striking points for your opponent. Occasionally, you will have to trade something on your wants list for another thing on your needs list. I will use a vacation as an example again because this is a time when several people's agendas have to blend together seamlessly. Nobody wants to argue throughout the trip because they're dissatisfied. When I go on vacation I need to be on a cruise ship because staying in hotels is something I do all the time as a professional speaker. I wouldn't feel like I could relax in a hotel, and I wouldn't want to do all that packing and unpacking. So my wife and I agree that we will go on a cruise every year, but she gets to pick the excursions we take at the various ports of call. This works out well because her need is to take in the history and the art of the location. My youngest son's only need is that the cruise have a "Kid's Club" where he can make new "best friends."

Only after you've identified your needs do you develop a list of wants. These are the things it would be nice to have, but they aren't crucial to your decision. In your next car, you might *like* leather seats, a global positioning system, and a CD player, but if the car was safe and it was the right price, you'd buy it anyway. Wants are the things you can part with, albeit reluctantly, to obtain, or retain, your needs. It is in your interest to identify as many wants as possible because these give you flexibility in negotiations. Brainstorm ahead of time so you can develop an extensive list. Use the Internet, make phone calls, or talk to others to make sure you're not leaving anything out.

It's important to be open and honest with yourself about both your wants and your needs. This doesn't mean you will always get them, but if you don't know what they are, you run into several problems: (1) You can't negotiate for something you're not aware of; (2) the other party cannot give something if you don't ask for it; (3) if you leave a discussion empty-handed while the other person got everything he or she wanted, you will probably bear resentment without realizing why. I have seen people seethe with resentment because the other person wasn't "considerate" enough to address their needs, when in reality the person just wasn't psychic enough to guess what those needs were.

If you can live without something, that's a want, not a need, and it can change, depending on a number of variables. In California, air-conditioning in a car might be a want, whereas in Arizona it would be a need. A swimming pool might be a want for most people, but for a family with a handicapped child whose only form of exercise is in a pool, it would obviously be a need. You have to examine your lists closely, though, to see how well you really understand yourself. Many of our "needs" actually turn out to be wants if we're really honest. Over the years I have heard people say such things as "I need a fur coat," "I need a Porsche," or "I need a big-screen television." These perks certainly do add a splash of flavor to our lives, but do we really need them? And yet, for some people, even these commodities could really be needs. A man who lives near the Arctic Circle truly needs a fur coat, a Porsche salesperson should probably be driving the same vehicle she's trying to sell, and someone who directs television programs probably needs to view them in the best format.

Too many people think only of saving money when negotiating. This is a mistake because there are many factors that outweigh cost, such as quality, reliability, and deliverability. Nordstrom sells men's and women's clothing at the going rate, but they attract customers because their service is so good. Lexus certainly does not make the cheapest cars on the market, but they are considered very reliable on the highway. And Federal Express charges a lot more than the post office, but it is renowned for its ability to deliver packages "absolutely, positively overnight," and they are true to that promise. What good is a low price if the product breaks after a week? How much of a bargain is it if you can't return it after it breaks? Is it really a good deal if the product arrives two days later than your deadline? Once I ordered special ceiling molding for a new chandelier I was having installed. I was willing to pay full price for the molding, but I was very clear that it had to be delivered within two days. So while I did not haggle over the price, I did negotiate for the dealer to truck it in especially for me at no additional cost. A price discount would have been useless if the molding had arrived after the chandelier was installed.

Believe it or not, sellers may not always need to receive the highest price, either. Often making a sale quickly or working with a competent buyer who will cut down the aggravation are more important benefits than receiving your asking price. The extra money won't compensate you if the deal takes much longer to consummate or it falls through entirely.

2. Set Goals in Advance

Once you have your list of wants and needs clearly defined, then it's time to set your goals, which are essentially all your needs and as many of your wants as you can think of, all packaged together. Needs, as we have said, represent the bare minimum you will accept. This is commonly known as your *bottom line*, which for buyers means the most you would pay and for sellers, the least you would accept. They are nonnegotiable. Your wants, however, can range from the ideal, perfect package, which includes everything, to your minimal group of wants.

For example, if you sold your house because you want to travel in your golden years, your need might be to purchase a recreational vehicle. You should decide ahead of time where you will drive your RV. If it will be around the southern states, make sure it has air-conditioning. If it is to Alaska, you want a good heater. If you have arthritis, you may want as many power features as possible, like steering and brakes.

Remember that there are other variables. Keep in mind that the RV is your need and so are some of the options, depending on what use you intend to make of the vehicle. Your goal is to get your need met, plus as many options as you can, and to pay the least amount possible. How well you're doing with that is your scorecard.

Set your goals high, yet be realistic. Women especially need to set their goals high because often they don't believe they deserve more. In *Women Don't Ask*, Babcock and Laschever say, "Many scholars believe that women are satisfied with less because they expect less. . . ." They also note, "Studies suggest that women as a rule expect to be paid less than men expect to be paid for the same work." A female lawyer once told me that she instructed her women clients to figure out an accurate figure when going for a settlement, and then double it. That's the only way they won't cheat themselves.

3. Anticipate Your Opponent's Wants and Needs

As we said, the striking points on your opponents are their needs. Like you, they will sacrifice some of their wants to protect their needs. It's important, before negotiations start, to actively anticipate what the other party's wants and needs will be because this will give you your negotiating range. Obviously, you will only really find out what they are when you're well into the bargaining session, but sometimes you can gain insight into what they're thinking by putting yourself in their shoes.

For example, let's say you want to pay a set price to have your yard work done. You might find out, by asking, that the gardener has plenty of work on weekends and little during the week, so he would appreciate being hired for a Wednesday. He might also prefer to use your garden tools so he doesn't have to drive his gas-guzzling truck to work. With a few well-timed and appropriate questions, you can negotiate a lower fee in exchange for making his work-week easier.

Remember that a negotiation is a give-and-take, and you can work with this. Always give the other side a little so you can score a few points yourself. But if you don't know what they value, you could be giving something that costs you dearly yet is worth virtually nothing to them. The only way you can know is to actively anticipate what their needs in this deal are.

4. Determine the Strength of Your Opponent's Needs and Wants

Martial artists are taught by a code of ethics to respond to a threat with an appropriate amount of force. If you are on the street and a drunken bully is trying to goad you into a fight, you may use only enough force to keep the bully away from you; this is known as a Level One response. If the bully grabs you to get your attention, then a Level Two response is warranted, which might mean throwing him to the ground. If he has a bat and wants your wallet, a Level Three response is required, which could mean you take the weapon away and perhaps even hit him with it. If he has a knife or a gun, you know he is desperate, so you should use a Level Four response, which means you will use possibly deadly force.

In negotiating, there are different levels of need and want that motivate both you and your opponent. As in martial arts, you should respond appropriately. You might be curious about how flexible the price of an item is and make a silly offer that has little chance of being accepted. In this case you almost hope the other party doesn't say yes because then you'll have to really consider the purchase. You might be interested in selling but not until later, in which case you are still not overly motivated to get involved in serious bargaining. Finally, you might be desperate, which means you have a strong need to make a deal. In this instance, you should guard your position but not lose the buyer or seller. The art is in not allowing opponents to see how much you want them to accept your offer, so the use of guile is essential in such cases. Just as you are making these decisions for yourself, you have to determine how motivated the other party is as well. Is the person itching to make a deal or just dancing with you? Perhaps you should wait until the person is serious before you put your cards on the table.

5. Hide Your Own Striking Points

From your very first day studying martial arts, you learn to protect your striking points with blocks, and you learn to take a stance that minimizes exposing them to an opponent. In negotiating you should learn as much as you can about your counterparts' wants and needs while keeping yours as close to the vest as possible. You are most certainly going to have to share some of them to build rapport and trust, as well as to encourage other parties to share theirs. However, keep the most important ones to yourself; otherwise, you become vulnerable.

It's like playing poker. Your aim is to maneuver your opponents into turning their cards over onto the table without having to do the same yourself. If you are looking to buy a large-screen television set, you might not tell the salesperson that you intend to buy a stereo surround sound system as well until you see the best price you can get on the TV. Then when you add in the stereo you would expect to get an even better deal on the whole package.

If you're the salesperson, you might explain the benefits of the extended warranty without revealing the dealer's profit margin. If customers know that it's big, they will try to take part of it away in the form of a lower price. You probably shouldn't reveal the size of your commission for the same reason.

DON'T FIXATE ON ANY ONE GOAL

When considering your opponent's striking points, don't get caught fixating on any one to the exclusion of others. If a chess player becomes obsessed with taking pawns, her opponent could be moving in on her queen and king. She is so eagerly gobbling up pawns that she takes her eyes off the bigger goal—to win the game. What good is holding all eight of your opponent's pawns if he now has your king?

Sometimes martial arts fighters concentrate so hard on just one spot that they can lose sight of their opponents' other weak points. One time while sparring, I scored big with a blow to my opponent's head. He became so focused on hitting me back in the head that he left himself open to numerous jabs to the body. As a result, I won the bout because I accumulated more points overall, while he was preoccupied with just one goal.

Here's an example of why you shouldn't obsess about any one aspect of a deal when negotiating. When I moved from San Francisco about thirty miles away to teach college, I didn't want to sell my house in San Francisco so I had only $10,000 in cash to buy a new home. Given this limited down payment, I knew that I could only buy using a lease-option agreement, which would allow me to rent the property while continuing to save up for the down payment. I found an owner who had not updated her home since the 1970s, and it therefore languished on the market with no offer, at a price of $550,000.

So I made an offer at $350,000 just to see how serious the seller was. Of course, my offer was rejected, but I did receive a counteroffer for $475,000, so I received a $75,000 price reduction for nothing. Making the offer also enabled me to meet and build rapport with the seller.

After two more months I made the seller another offer of $375,000, hoping she had become more realistic. She looked at the offer, got red in the face, slammed her fist on the table, and shouted, "$425,000! Take it or leave it!"

It became clear to me that she just wanted to be able to tell her friends that she got "over $400,000" like they did. So I said I would think about it, and I rewrote my offer as a lease option for $425,000 with only $10,000 down to hold the property for two years. If I bought the house, the seller would add this to my down payment, and if not, she could keep it and I would move out. I would also pay $3,000 a month in rent, but half would be credited each month toward my down payment if I exercised the lease option. In addition, I got the seller to agree to carry the loan for seven years using an *interest-only* loan so my payments on an expensive house were relatively low.

The result was that after two years of "renting," I was able to buy the property thanks to the terms of our deal, which enabled me to save up enough money for the down payment and gave me affordable mortgage payments. Because the seller was focused solely on the price, I was able to name the terms, which were much more important to me. Without the right terms I could never have purchased this home with only $10,000 cash in a hot real estate market.

So before you sit down at the bargaining table, make a list of your needs and wants. Have clear goals for what you want out of the negotiation and stick to them. Next, try to anticipate the same thing for your opponent. Above all, don't fixate on any one goal for too long, or it could make you vulnerable to attacks by your opponent.

YELLOW BELT TEST

Before receiving a yellow belt, martial artists must demonstrate the ability to kick and block kicks. Prior to your receiving a yellow belt in negotiating, you must answer the following:

1. What are the rules of power and how are they used?
2. Why is spying on your opponent so crucial to negotiators?
3. Name three sources of information that could help you with your next major negotiation.
4. Why is interviewing such a powerful spying technique?
5. Complete this sentence: "The quality of the _____ determines the quality of the _____."
6. Why do women tend to be more adept at asking questions than men?
7. Why do people like answering questions?

8. Why are people more likely to truthfully answer open questions than closed?
9. Why should you spend more time doing research when considering larger transactions?
10. Why is discovering background information about a company important to effective negotiations?
11. Why is the location in which you will be negotiating important?
12. What is the difference between a need and a want?
13. What are your opponent's striking points in a negotiation?
14. Why is making a written list of your needs and wants so crucial?
15. Why should you set goals before the negotiation has even begun?
16. Name three things that can be as important as money in a transaction?
17. Why is it important to anticipate your opponent's needs and wants?
18. Why should you know the strength of your opponent's needs and wants?
19. Why do you need to reveal some of your striking points?
20. Why should you not fixate on any one goal?

Exercise

Now it's time to engage in your first contest. Don't worry—it will be a safe one. The next time you are at a friend's house, ask the person to think of an item he or she has lying around that could be sold at a garage sale. Next, use some of the techniques you've learned so far to begin negotiations on that spare couch, coffee table, or television set.

Obviously, if you are truly interested in what the friend has for sale, you are certainly welcome to buy it. If not, you've helped your friend come up with a reasonable price for the item.

Be sure to ask the following questions before you begin to bargain:

1. Is there anything you've been thinking of selling at a garage or rummage sale? (If not, visit another friend until you find someone who has unwanted items lying around.)
2. Why would you want to sell it?
3. How much do you think you'd be willing to sell it for?
4. Would you take . . . ? (Name a price well below the asking price.)

Postexercise Debrief

Immediately following this exercise answer the following questions:

1. What did you learn about your friend's reason for selling?
2. Did this information give you an advantage during the bargaining process?
3. Which of the rules of power did you employ?
4. Were you able to keep the "most important question" in mind?
5. Were you able to separate your needs from your wants?
6. Did you have a clear goal for the price you wanted to pay?
7. What would you do differently now that the negotiation is over?
8. Which rule of power would you like to learn more about?
9. What would you say was your greatest strength during this negotiation?
10. How do you now feel about negotiating?

You'll notice that even during this exercise, you saw a number of principles from this book in action. First of all, you were cunning in that you didn't tell your friend your real motive for asking these questions. I'm sure you saw leverage moving back and forth as your friend began to recognize that you might be interested in the item. You got to see rather common objections to any low offer. You probably wished you had been able to conduct research before the negotiations began. Finally, you got to see how wants and needs work in the bargaining process.

The reason you were instructed to choose a friend for this exercise is that it gave you a negotiating experience without having to deal with the additional challenges that come from bargaining with a perfect stranger. With someone you don't know, you have absolutely no rapport, no trust, and no relationship to build upon. You are, in effect, starting from scratch. You must take steps to get to know this person better before you can really launch a negotiating strategy. This will come next, in Chapter 7, "Developing the Fighting Stance."

PART III

Green Belt

The sprout becomes a seedling that begins
to develop and grow in strength.

A t this stage, students have established basic skills and now they are put into practice in the ring. It's time to demonstrate what they've been learning with sparring.

In Chapter 7—"Developing the Fighting Stance"—students learn that how they strike a fighting pose telegraphs what kind of fighter they are—competent or frightened? As they grow stronger at the green belt level, they have to let the other side see their confidence. The fighting stance communicates a great deal. Negotiators are also broadcasting their readiness to the person across the table and this chapter details how to communicate the right things.

As they begin sparring, most new students simply copy each other because, when they do, they limit what their opponent is capable of throwing from any particular stance. If their opponent kicks and they return it they will only exchange kicks until someone moves in to punching distance. In Chapter 8—"Opening Tactics"—negotiators will learn how to *mirror* the other party to put them at ease and share information; this is crucial to both sides. Just as a fighter jabs to see what kind of response they can elicit, you will learn how to throw offers onto the table designed to get your opponent to tip his or her hand.

Once a fighter responds to a jab a martial artist learns to use that reaction to read his opponent and assess his qualities. When sparring, fighters know they can be hurt so they want to be hyperaware of how good their nemesis is. And so in Chapter 9—"Reading Your Opponent"—begins the art of observation. You will learn that people fall under four basic categories of personality, and finding what type the person you are bargaining with is adds a new weapon to the arsenal. One tiny signal can broadcast a heap of useful information.

7

Developing the Fighting Stance

Your opening stance can set the tone
for successful negotiations.
MICHAEL SOON LEE

Chapter 6 explored the importance of assessing both the subtle and the obvious striking points of your opponent, while at the same time keeping yours as invisible as possible. Now we're going to examine what to do just before the match and right at the beginning of the match.

Once martial artists have learned the fundamentals and done their homework on practice bags, it's time for them to actually meet real opponents. However, as we said earlier, before sparring begins you must stretch your muscles. Besides limbering you up, this also enables you to assess your physical condition. Are you loose or tight? Are you warm or cold? Are you ready to fight?

Next, you walk onto the mat and bow to your opponent as a sign of respect, and then you take your fighting stance. In martial arts this is called the *on-guard position*. This is the stance you take before beginning to spar. It tells your partner that you are ready. The stance you take also tells your opponent a lot more—what style of martial arts you practice, how much skill you have developed, and how much confidence you have. The on-guard position must be strong and allow you to strike quickly. You are like a coiled spring that appears to be at rest but can release its energy instantly.

In negotiating, you must warm up by greeting your opponent and then establish an on-guard position. In bargaining, this is your demeanor when you first meet your bargaining partner and begin to throw offers onto the table. Your posture will change during the contest, but you should always take an initial stance with purpose and forethought. It helps set the tone for a positive outcome for both parties because, done properly, it can put your opponent at ease and into a more receptive state of mind.

Before you even begin to take a stance, though, you need to be aware of a few important principles that form the foundation of learning how to meet an opponent head-on. To develop an effective negotiating stance you must always start by evaluating your physical condition. Martial artists must make sure they are in top fighting shape before a match. They will get plenty of sleep the night before, eat a high-protein meal several hours in advance of the contest, and warm up just enough to loosen all the muscles but not so much that they make themselves tired.

Negotiators must also be in top condition both physically and mentally because bargaining is stressful on the mind as well as the body. You should eat a light, nutritious meal just before the meeting so you have enough food to absorb stomach acid; if you don't, you could become uncomfortable just when bargaining reaches a crucial point. Your own discomfort will unsettle you and could tip the table in your opponent's favor. Always try to arrange to bargain when you're at your best. If you're more alert in the morning, schedule the session for that time of day. If you are an afternoon or evening person, set the time for after lunch. Aim for when you are at your peak.

Are there certain foods that increase your sharpness or focus? Maybe you need coffee or chocolate. Are there certain foods or drinks that make you dull or sleepy? Some of us are just not at our best after a heavy meal. Obviously, even though some believe it relaxes them, drinking alcohol is a sure way to dull your senses.

Next, you have to decide how open to be with the other party. In other words, how much can you disclose without hurting your own position?

Being open builds trust and makes your opponent more likely to feel comfortable giving you valuable information. Obviously, it's important not to be too open, but you often need to share information that is of interest to both sides in order to see the lay of the land and find out how this deal can help both parties.

Be sure that when you start talking, you don't make promises you can't keep, or you will lose trust and credibility. It's usually best to strive to under-promise and overdeliver, which builds trust and reliance.

Even though you are in opposition to the other party, you should still put the person at ease before entering the transaction. Remember that negotiating can be stressful for a lot of people. The more you can relieve stress, the better it will be all around. In the martial arts, the on-guard position makes an opponent feel comfortable not only because it is expected, but also because it tells the opponent that you are a capable and trained practitioner. Experienced negotiators can also put their opponents at ease by their stance.

Your initial demeanor should make your counterpart feel relaxed. It may seem as if you are helping out the other side, but there is an old saying: "People do business with people they like." If opponents like you, they may give you a better deal than they had intended. Being likable works in your favor and often keeps the other party from being overly aggressive. It's harder to attack someone toward whom you feel friendly.

Black belt negotiators can disarm their opponents by just smiling. A well-timed and genuine smile can relax your bargaining partners. It implies that there is nothing to be concerned about in the impending activity. It can also make opponents wonder what you're up to or what you know that they don't know.

Next, you may want to shake hands with your bargaining partner before you begin, to establish a note of civility. However, be aware that not all people want to shake hands, particularly women who are new immigrants. For some—for example, traditional Japanese, Asian, Orthodox Jews, Indian, and Muslim women—this could be very offensive to their beliefs and traditions. Instead of assuming, let them take the lead. If they are comfortable with this practice, they will extend their hand to you. If not, simply nod to show respect.

Having a peaceful, almost serene look on your face also puts other people at ease. To do this, your face must be relaxed and open. I know it will look weird, but before you enter the bargaining room, scrunch up your face as tight as it will go and then just let all the muscles relax. When you walk in, any tension in your face will be gone. Just don't enter the room with your face still puckered up, or things may not go so well!

It is not only your outward appearance that is important. What goes on in your mind also counts. Try to think positive thoughts so that you generate and radiate positive energy. Such thoughts could include imagining a successful outcome to the negotiations, the possibility of making a new friend, and the opportunity to get a great deal on some item you want or obtaining the best price possible on an item you are selling. You may find it helpful to repeat positive affirmations such as "I know they will accept my offer," "We can put this deal together," or "There are many good reasons why this agreement benefits both of us."

Positive energy is contagious. Have you noticed that when someone smiles at you on the street, you automatically smile back? You can have the same positive impact on the person you are bargaining with. Don't we all like being around positive people? Positive thoughts, words, and attitudes can call forth positive moods and actions, including accepting an offer we otherwise might not have.

Conversely, a negative attitude can easily transfer to those around you. Have you ever watched a jovial mood suddenly turn sour when a negative person enters the room? It's like throwing a bucket of cold water on the occasion. In fact, there's a saying that such people can brighten an entire room—just by leaving. So choose to be positive.

If you want to emulate experienced martial artists, practice *mushin,* which means totally emptying your mind and allowing your training to take over. Bruce Lee said, "The great mistake is to anticipate the outcome of the engagement; you ought not to be thinking of whether it ends in victory or defeat. Let nature takes its course, and your tools will strike at the right moment." Bruce was talking about not worrying about winning or losing while you're in the heat of the battle because it can be a distraction. Obviously, before he ever entered a contest he set his full intention on winning. This was true not only for martial arts but for his movie career as well.

When you're negotiating, you must also practice *mushin*; otherwise, you could taint the proceedings from the start with your preconceptions. I once went into a negotiation with what I thought was damaging information about the other party. As a result, I started out very aggressively and with a rather accusatory attitude toward my counterpart. When my information turned out to be wrong, I never recovered from the negative tone my initial assumption had set.

It's best to remove from your consciousness any emotional residue and unyielding reactions. Avoid assumptions about yourself or others. Don't assume you know what's going to happen before it does. Try not to second-guess the other person's motivations or intentions.

It's especially important not to make negative assumptions because this could cause you to underestimate the person. It's easy to assume that just because someone is relatively young or a woman she may not be a competent negotiator. You could be very wrong about that. However, don't assume that just because someone comes from a negotiating country like China or Mexico, he is automatically going to be a tough bargainer. He might actually be rather timid and tentative.

We've already discussed making your opponent feel comfortable. Another facet of that is tone of voice, not just because a relaxed tone brings a peaceful atmosphere, but because an even tone will mask any tension you might feel that you don't want the other party to know about. Martial artists will yell to intimidate their opponents, but unfortunately it can give their opponents the edge because they can tell how much stress the yellers are under just by the sound of their voices. At the negotiation table, too, your voice can disclose your state of mind. A person who is under stress will sound high-pitched, shrill, and disturbing, so it's important not to communicate that.

Negotiators use their voices in exactly the opposite way that martial artists do. They refrain from ever yelling and instead seek a voice level that is relaxed, low, soothing, and calming to the other party. It helps to dissipate any distress or anger the person might be feeling that could derail the talks.

Concentrate on relaxing your voice by yawning a couple of times and, as you exhale, say *aaahhhh*. Notice how your throat relaxes and your voice deepens and softens. When you speak, you should feel a subtle vibration in your nose and mouth area, which tells you that your voice is tranquil. A calm tone is soothing and almost mesmerizing. Again, this can help to calm the many tense situations that can arise in the bargaining process.

Although you should avoid giving away any information about yourself through tone of voice, you certainly should try to pick up as much data about the other party as you can. Your opponent's stance can tell you a lot. That's why in a tournament the first thing martial artists do is note their opponent's stance before the contest begins. Is most of the opponent's weight on the front or back foot or to the side? How far apart are the feet? These observations can give you a clue about the opponent's preferred fighting style and dictate the moves that can and cannot be done from that stance.

The stance can also indicate another person's level of confidence and experience. Your opponent's guarded position is usually his or her strength. In most cases, the closer the hands are to the body, the more likely the opponent is to throw a punch. If the hands are out in front, the more likely the person is to use them to parry or block.

Novice negotiators may be timid or unsure and will tend to reflect this in their body language. They may sit a bit hunched over, avoid eye contact, or smile uneasily. Try not to assume too much by this, though, since there are some pretty good actors in the world of negotiating who will deliberately use this tactic to lure you into letting down your guard. Just make a mental note about the person's demeanor and see if there is consistency throughout the bargaining process. A person who really is timid will retain the posture throughout; one who is faking will forget to keep up the pose once in a while.

After the initial greeting, a black belt negotiator *should* take an open stance, because it implies confidence and honesty, with nothing to hide. It generally requires squarely facing the opponent with your arms uncrossed and your hands open. Martial artists who open themselves up in this way show either supreme confidence or foolhardiness. Bruce Lee would sometimes drop his hands to his sides in front of a whole group of armed attackers as if to say, "You can't touch me." I advocate this when bargaining because it encourages the other party to be just as open as you.

The negotiating stance is calm but also upright and alert, with the practitioner always looking for openings and opportunities. Again, the expression on your face should be calm, almost peaceful looking. If you begin with an open posture, it encourages the other party to be equally open with any information he or she has to share.

The open posture, above all, invites trust, which is essential. That is why, at the beginning of any contest, martial artists always bow to each other as a sign of respect and trust. At the start of any negotiation, you want to build trust with the opposing party. This makes the person more open to sharing vital information and more willing to do a deal with you.

Asking questions and disclosing important information helps to build trust at the bargaining table. Remember how this was done earlier.

Women are often masters at building trust. Just as many people assume that men are holding something back, they think that women are being open and forthcoming. If you are a woman, be aware of this fact because you can make it work for you. For instance, women who have jobs in traditionally male fields like remodeling are more likely to be trusted than men, and they can play that up when marketing themselves.

Real trust also comes from internal integrity—in other words, being yourself instead of what you think a negotiator should act like. This is why it's important to be authentic in a negotiation. It leaves you far more grounded than if you're putting on an act, as you have to expend energy to keep an act going. It doesn't take any effort to be you.

What makes top martial artists successful is that they take the same basic training as everyone else, but then they add their own own style to it. Bruce Lee was not the first or only practitioner of Wing Chung kung fu, but the minute you saw him in the movies or on television you instantly knew it was him, even if he was in a darkened room. He was uniquely himself, and there was no one else like him.

When I negotiate in many different types of situations, I bring my own unique sense of humor, caring, and focus to the table, along with my experience. Many people have commented that they appreciated my genuineness when bargaining. You've got to be yourself in negotiations.

However, having said that, if one of the natural qualities that you manifest is timidity, you might want to develop a healthy dose of confidence to combat it because it won't serve you in a negotiation. Confidence is inside you—it only has to be nurtured to come alive. Martial artists must be confident, or they would never step into the ring. However, a big part of Asian philosophy is humility. So what's the difference between confidence and cockiness? Basically, when you have confidence, you know you are capable because of your training and well-developed skill. People who are cocky claim far more than they can deliver. They possess a kind of arrogance and can't stop telling people how good they are. If you are certain about your abilities, there is no need to talk about them. It reminds me of people I know who are always bragging about how honest they are. If they're so honest, why do they need to say so? It makes you wonder.

Obviously, it's important to be confident during negotiations because it assures the other party that you know what you're doing and makes the person more willing to go along with many of your suggestions. However, don't let your confidence turn into arrogance, because people hate arrogance. They often go out of their way to bring down those who display this trait.

Bruce Lee said that a relaxed posture and deep breathing enable one to maintain a "poker body," a body that reveals no more of its intended movements than a "poker face" reveals the cards a player holds. You let loose no outward signs—called *tells*—about what you are feeling or what your move will be. In addition, being calm on the outside allows you to be fully alert on the inside.

In the beginning, your negotiating posture must be practiced consciously until such time as it becomes subconscious. This may take weeks or years. Do not assume you know how you look. You could be giving away information about your state of mind without knowing it. Use a mirror to make sure this is the image you really want to project.

Don't be obvious with your stance. The important point for martial artists is not to have a classical "get set" posture or preparatory movements prior to delivering the straight punch—or any punch, for that matter. Having a "get set" posture is like wearing a sandwich board that announces what you're going to do next. Bruce Lee said, "The leading straight punch is delivered from your ready stance without any added motions like drawing your hand back to your hip or shoulder, pulling back your shoulder, etc."

And finally, vary your posture so you do not become tired and so your intentions are not obvious to the other person. Yet you must still remember to stay open to the other party so that you convey a sense of confidence and friendliness.

8

Opening Tactics

Start every contest on the right footing.
SENSEI TABUCHI

How you start a contest is crucial to winning or losing. When martial artists are fighting someone they know, it can actually be harder because each of them is familiar with the other's tendencies. A friend is someone with whom you feel comfortable, so there's no need to do much sparring because you've built a relationship over a long period of time. What's not so easy is the fact that the friend knows your tendencies and weaknesses and will try to exploit them. However, you know your friend's style and vital striking points as well. It is very difficult to win a contest with a friend because you have to come up with something completely new and different in order to prevail. You also will feel bad if the friend loses, although your competitive nature will probably take care of that. You just don't want to humiliate your friend, or vice versa.

When you are fighting a stranger, though, you know nothing about each other and there is no need to be original. The downside is that you also don't know if this is a person who will really try to hurt you, and you are clueless about their tactics. It's a real mystery. However, you have no problem hitting this stranger with everything you've got and even basking in the glory of victory. The reason people become our friends in the first place is that we know what kind of people they are and we already find their character acceptable. We regard them as trustworthy.

So before starting any bargaining session with someone you don't know, break the ice by building rapport. The dictionary defines *rapport* as "a relationship marked by harmony, conformity, accord, or affinity." It is the art of developing cooperation and trust between you and another person by finding similarities and building on them.

An ancient Chinese proverb says, "People who *are like* each other, like each other." Remember that the other party may be feeling defensive, confrontational, or apprehensive. Finding a common bond puts them at ease and helps them open to you in a way that is almost magical.

The easiest way to build rapport is to talk about anything *except* the subject of your negotiations. Instead of launching right into the business at hand, take time to get to know each other; build rapport by chatting because it establishes relationship. It's easier for people to buy or sell with those with whom they have begun to feel empathy and trust.

Building rapport can be like love at first sight or it can take a lot of time to develop. In most cases, you must take the time to build it. One way is to focus solely on the other person and use his or her name often. Ask about hobbies, sports, favorite movies or books, and the person's family. Pay sincere compliments about their interests and achievements as you search for a connection. The ensuing discussion is not merely idle chitchat but something that will help you learn the person's needs and wants. Once you discover an area of mutual interest, slowly bring the focus onto the subject at hand.

For example, if you're selling a pair of used water skis, you might talk about your mutual interest in water sports in general and then eventually ask more specific questions, such as how long the potential buyer has been skiing, where the person likes to ski, what kind of towboat he or she plans to use, and other related questions. This is an obvious line of questioning, since the subject of your negotiations readily lends itself to water skiing. However, often there is less of an obvious tie-in, so you have to work a bit harder to find commonality. If you get stuck for a question, you can always fall back on one of the five *w*'s of newspaper reporting by asking "Who?," "What?," "When?," "Where?," or "Why?"

At the beginning of a martial arts tournament, you must mirror your opponent, matching your energy with that of the other person. Even if the person does something sudden, like give you a loud yell, you would do the same, but come back with an even louder shout. Not making these comebacks not only fails to establish congruence, it could be taken as a sign of weakness. We call this practice *mirroring* because it produces the same experience as moving around in front of a mirror and seeing the image do the same thing. Later in the match you should break away from mirroring because it's hard to score points when you are matching your opponent. However, until you feel comfortable with the other person's capabilities, it's the safest thing to do. You might not be able to score while mirroring, but neither can your opponent, and the advantages at this stage are worth the effort.

In a negotiation, it is important to match an opponent's energy, focus, and intensity because, like building rapport, this will make the person more receptive to your offer. Instead of seeing you as foreign and someone to be wary of, the other party will view you as more of a friend, as "one of us," because there is a subconscious comfort level.

During the opening exploratory period, you should particularly note the other person's body language and rate of speech. Is the person sitting upright and alert or is the posture more laid-back and relaxed? Does the person speak fast or slow? In my experience, people from New York tend to speak more quickly, while someone from Berlin talks more deliberately, and someone from the American South generally has a slower cadence. Once you've noticed these characteristics, your aim is to copy the body language, rate of speech, energy level, and even breathing pattern, without being too obvious. The last thing you should do is look like you're making fun of the person. Mirroring the other party physically and verbally reinforces the subconscious message that "we have something in common."

Studies in neurolinguistic programming (NLP) indicate that information is communicated 55 percent through body language, 38 percent through tone of voice, and only 7 percent through the actual words spoken. What NLP suggests is that you can build rapport until it becomes natural. To do this, you will need to match these characteristics:

- Voice tonality (how you sound) or speed
- Breathing rates
- Rhythm of movement and energy levels
- Body postures and gestures

You also should try to match the person's preferred learning style. People gather information in one of three ways: verbally, kinesthetically, or visually. By presenting data in a way that the other person can best take in, first, you endear yourself to the person and, second, you facilitate the entire process of communication. We tend to assume that others learn using the same mode we do, but actually their styles can be quite different.

Hearing people say certain phrases can be a clue to their preferred learning style. Auditory communicators prefer receiving information verbally and may say things such as "The deal sounds good to me" and "I hear what you are saying." If you are referring to a place on the map and the person has it upside down, you know it's time to switch to verbal instructions.

Visual communicators prefer to absorb information when looking at pictures, charts, and graphs. You may hear them say something like "The deal looks like it could work" or "I see what you are saying." If you're demonstrating how to do something and they still have a puzzled look on their face, try using a chart or diagram.

Kinesthetic communicators prefer to examine objects physically or visit sites to gain firsthand experience. They may say phrases such as "This feels good to me" or "I can grasp that concept." With this group, try demonstrating what you mean.

We began this chapter with the idea of exploring your opponent; now it is time to test the person. When martial artists start to spar, the first thing they generally do is throw a few jabs at their partner just to warm up and see what kind of response they receive. People who constantly tense up might be projecting that they are tentative and fearful. People who simply smile and look relaxed project confidence.

One way negotiators test their opponents is to make offers and ask for more in the deal than they expect to receive. The person's reaction will tell you if that offer is on track or way off base, and then you can adjust your next moves to coincide with this new information. If a seller shows shock and anger at an offer, it could be because he or she is not privy to some piece of information that justifies a low price. You might have to produce data showing that you had good reason to make that offer. If the person still doesn't budge in spite of all the evidence, then you might be embarking on an impossible mission that is going nowhere fast. It could be time to move on.

When sellers quote a price, they are actively looking for a response to see if buyers are willing to pay that price. Buyers who show no negative reaction at all aren't handing the seller usable information and, in fact, might be giving misinformation. The seller might assume that the person's lack of response means he or she is willing to pay full price, and then the seller will not come down much at all as talks progress. In fact, the seller may even try to get you to pay extra for options that would otherwise have been thrown in for free. As we can see, testing your opponent also means letting yourself be tested.

Men do not have much trouble asking for what they want, or even more than they expect, with their first offer. For many women, however, this can be a tough thing to do. Studies show that women tend to be afraid of shocking or disappointing others by being too bold or demanding. The last thing a timid woman wants to do is ask for more than she expects to receive, more than she believes she *should* receive, because this might cause the other party to back off and be offended. To avoid this reaction, she may just pay full price. Again, with practice, women can learn to ask for more than what they want as well as any man. All they are really doing with their offer is testing the waters.

This might surprise you, but after making an offer, there is one response a black belt negotiator *never* wants to hear, and that is the word *okay.* Quite simply, hearing okay means that you could have done better. You just weren't aggressive enough. This is another reason you should always ask for more than you expect to get. If you have to come down some, that's fine.

In the beginning of a bargaining session, you are both getting your toes wet. Everybody wants to get along, and they're all on their best behavior. They are relaxed at this point and haven't really begun to fight. In my experience, this is when people are the most truthful, so it is the perfect time to find out what the truth looks like in your opponent; then you have something to match future behavior against. After a while, when you start to squeeze them to win points, they have more of an incentive to lie. Later in the book, we will find out what a lie looks like, but first we must learn to recognize what the truth looks like.

This is the time to observe the other party being truthful, so you have a yardstick to measure against. Just as a lie detector technician starts an interrogation by asking very simple questions like name, birth date, and occupation to obtain a baseline of true and false answers from a suspect, you should begin negotiations by asking questions you know will be answered truthfully. Carefully observe the body language, breathing pattern, and facial tension. Listen to the rate of speech and the voice pitch. If the person varies from this behavior later, you can tell he or she is prevaricating.

Here are some truth-eliciting questions buyers might ask of sellers:

- Are you the person I spoke with over the phone?
- How much did you say you wanted for this?
- Did I see an ad in the newspaper (or appropriate media)?

- Who's the manufacturer again?
- Which model is this?
- What color does this look like to you?

Here are some truth-eliciting questions sellers might ask of buyers:

- Are you the person I talked to over the phone?
- How do you spell your name?
- I believe you said you were looking for this in red (or other color)?
- What size do you normally wear?
- Were you planning on paying cash or charging?
- Are you buying this for yourself?

When you ask questions that you know are being answered truthfully, it tells you not only what the truth looks like but what it sounds like as well. In Chapter 10, you'll see how to spot when someone is being less than truthful.

You know that you have to share information, but what is the rule of thumb for *what* to share? It's easy: Share information that is important to both parties yet doesn't hurt your own position. This helps to build the trust and rapport you need to avoid unnecessary roadblocks later. A guideline for what kind of information you have to share is as follows: (1) anything they will find out anyway, (2) any facts they absolutely need to make a decision, and (3) anything that doesn't weaken your bargaining power.

This practice helps the other party understand your position and you to understand his. The art is in knowing what you can share and what you should keep private. For example, if you are negotiating with a contractor right after your house has been through a disaster, you need to tell him the age of the house, the kind of damage it sustained, and where the work needs to be done. Information that you absolutely don't want to share is that you pretty much have to take his bid because every contractor you've called is busy or that the other bids you received were scandalously high. That would allow him to quote you a price 20 percent over the normal cost of the job, knowing that he's still lower than the others. You also shouldn't tell him something that would discourage him from taking the job at all—for example, "This old house is really difficult to work on and most carpenters hate it."

Men and women differ in how much they educate the other party and in how they share information. Sensei Tabuchi says that male martial arts teachers tend to jump right into a lesson and explain how a move is to be executed. Female teachers are more likely to talk about the reason behind the move and explain why the move works before they teach the actual technique. This tends to be true in a negotiation as well. Men go straight to the point and begin throwing out offers, while women sellers tend to talk about the history of the piece and female buyers talk about how they plan to use it.

The following are just a few of the common differences between male and female negotiators:

- Males are usually more bottom-line-oriented (the "what"), whereas women want to know the reason for a proposal (the "why").
- Men often move more quickly and impulsively from one point to another, while women move more slowly and thoughtfully.
- Men tend to view negotiations as more win/lose while women are more collaborative.
- Men usually assume they know what the other party wants, whereas women tend to be more open to learning.
- Men regularly focus on outcomes, while women focus on relationships.
- Men often ask for what they want, whereas women ask for what they need.
- Men tend to set high goals, while women set more modest goals. In fact, a 2003 study entitled *Gender as a Situational Phenomenon in Negotiation* revealed that men typically set goals for negotiations that are 15 percent higher than those set by women.

Obviously, these statements will not always hold true, but be sure to watch for any of these tendencies to appear. If they do, you can plan your counter-moves based on this information.

One final note: In addition to the personal, individual information and limitations indicated here, it is also necessary to disclose basic characteristics and attributes of the object or service being sold. Of course, there's a real gray area here. How much do you have to tell your opponent and how much can you hold back? What is told and what is kept hidden depends largely on your level of honesty, your negotiating savvy, and possibly legal requirements.

Some of the information you share should make the other party emotionally attached to you. If the person feels emotionally involved, it can cause them to sell to or buy from you even though there are better deals on the table. For instance, when I'm presenting an offer for a homebuyer and I know there are other offers being submitted at the same time, I will often bring photographs of my clients to make the deal up close and personal. One time I noticed that a home seller had a picture of himself in a military uniform on the wall of his office. When going through my own buyers' photo album, I noticed a similar picture of the husband. We were competing with seven other prospective buyers, so I slipped the military photo among the really cute shots of my clients camping and at the beach. When the seller reached this picture in the stack, he exclaimed, "Ah, a military man. Good man." He sold the house to us even though ours was not the highest offer in the group because I used a picture to create an emotional bond with the buyer. Once you engage the opposing party on a deep level, the person is more likely to give you what you want because emotions build rapport faster than anything else.

At some point in the course of conversing and sharing information, one of you has to make a move toward presenting an offer. When sparring in the dojo, it's usually best if the other person makes the first move. Jabbing is a move in martial arts that is designed to force the other side to commit first. It's a fake punch that is just meant to provoke a reaction and see how fast and aggressive your opponent is. It also lets you see what style the person practices and many other important factors.

When negotiating, you also want the other side to commit first. Here's why: When a buyer makes an offer on something you are selling, no matter how low it is initially, she can go in only one direction from there—up. Conversely, the minute a seller quotes a price on something you are interested in buying, he can go in only one direction from there—down. Either way, whether you are buying or selling, you want to the other person to quote the price first; that person is now in a weakened position because the only way he or she can now go is one that favors you.

In nonnegotiating countries, in most stores and offices it might not even occur to you to bargain. For instance, when you're shopping in a retail store and prices are clearly marked, that seems to imply that they aren't negotiable. Sometimes that's true. Sales clerks usually don't have the authority to hash it out with you (but someone else might). However, there are exceptions. First, if the store is owned by someone from a negotiating culture, that price tag may be considered only a starting point that is open to challenge. Second, that shopkeeper may not have intended to bargain, but after all, a sale is a sale. If you present an offer, the shopkeeper may go for it. Third, what most of us don't know is that virtually every store manager is empowered with the ability to automatically give 10 to 15 percent off just to keep from losing a sale.

Let's say you're looking to buy an expensive watch at a fine jewelry store. How do you get the seller to commit first when the price is prominently displayed? First, ask the salesperson an open-ended question like "What's the best price you can give me?" You'd be amazed how negotiable most supposedly fixed-price items are. Most of the time I am told, "The best we can do is give you a ten percent discount." Most people would gladly accept such a generous offer, but to me they've already dropped the price and I'm just getting started. Now I know the price is somewhat negotiable. Plus, the salesperson knows I'm interested and is moving into a negotiating frame of mind.

If you're selling an item, you want buyers to reveal to you that they're not just looking. This allows you to concentrate only on the serious customers. In sales, success is all about being efficient with your time. So when you're selling an item, get the buyer to commit first by making an offer—any offer. How close the offer is to your asking price is an indication of how interested and serious the buyer is or whether he or she is "just fishing." Now, no matter how low the offer is, the buyer must come up in price to stay in the game.

When negotiating with your spouse or children, it's really critical to get them to commit first because they might actually ask for less than you thought you had to give. If your teenager says she wants a later curfew, for example, don't right away pipe up and say, "How about eleven o'clock?" Instead, say, "What time do you think?" She might say, "Ten o'clock," and then you've just won yourself an extra hour. If you make the first offer, you set the bar high and then can't lower it. Only she can—and she won't.

What if you are a seller, and the buyer tries to get you to make the first offer by asking if you'd come down in price? Simply counter this move by being noncommittal and saying something like "Make me an offer; I won't be offended." The key is to encourage the buyer to make an offer, because until then, negotiations cannot even begin.

There are times, however, when you must commit first, whether you are buying or selling. In this instance you must always ask for more than you expect to receive because this leaves room for negotiation. If you're selling an antique cabinet, there can be a wide price range, depending on age, condition, demand, and rarity of the piece. Why not price it at the high end so you have lots of wiggle room? Remember, buyers are never going to *up* your offer, they're only going down. As always, there are exceptions to every rule, and we'll talk about that shortly.

If you are the buyer, of course, start at the low end of the range. For instance, when purchasing a home, the buyer is usually expected to make the first offer. However, there's no law that says you can't ask the seller or the seller's agent how flexible the price might be before you write a contract. Also, be aggressive with the price you offer unless you are competing with several other purchasers for a property you really want.

DON'T BE RIDICULOUS!

Although you should ask for more than you think the other party will accept, use your initial research to make sure there is some chance of success by presenting an offer that is at least within reason, even though it pushes the limits. There are a number of reasons that you shouldn't be ridiculous with your proposals:

1. You don't want to make the other party angry. A low yet reasonable offer to buy a boat may bring a smile to the seller's lips, but a ridiculous offer may cause the seller to throw you overboard.
2. You don't want to insult the other party. If you cause the other person to lose face, he or she will probably walk away and not deal with you again.
3. A silly offer implies that you aren't a serious person. Once this happens, your credibility will be ruined and the other party will be hard-pressed to take anything you say or do seriously. The person might refuse to entertain any future offers from you no matter how much you raise your price.

4. An unrealistic proposal says that you are unsophisticated and not a real player. This impression will taint the rest of your negotiation and cause the other party to doubt the benefit of even a brilliant suggestion.

Any one of these mistakes could cause other parties to believe you are wasting their time, and they won't want to deal with you. You must strike a balance between being optimistic and being realistic.

So how do you know what's reasonable? This goes back to spying on your opponent before you ever engage. You should lead into the negotiations with a range in mind from low to high that you will sell or buy for. Experienced sellers usually end up with the higher end of the range, and savvy buyers often pay the lower end of the scale.

The amount of resistance you receive to your offer will tell you a lot about your opponent. If you feel strong resistance to your initial offer, it could mean the other party is probably emotionally attached to the outcome or to the item in question. However, if you receive no resistance, the person either doesn't care about the subject of the negotiations or wants to throw you off track.

Many people from negotiating cultures make an initial offer that would embarrass most novice negotiators. In these countries, however, they don't recognize the term, because experienced negotiators are not embarrassed by any offer they make or receive. It's just a starting point, but it definitely says that the game has begun.

Whenever you are dealing with an item that you are unfamiliar with, you must be cautious. When buying, the less you *know* about the deal and the other party, the further your offer should be from the asking price. This protects you from paying more than it is worth in the face of not knowing what to pay. For instance, if you're looking at a painting by a relatively unknown artist, make sure you pay on the low end, since you can't be sure when it will appreciate, if ever, as opposed to one done by a well-known painter for whom there is a strong market. When selling, the less you know about the object or the current market, the *lower* you should actually go with your price. Although this contradicts what I said earlier about usually asking the higher end of the price range, remember who sets the price—buyers. For example, if you have a unique sailing schooner that you built from the keel up, you should price it low, sell it at an auction, and market it like crazy. The lower price tag should entice more buyers to compete with each other. The more bidders you attract, the greater the chance that there will be a bidding war. If you are afraid this feeding frenzy won't occur, be sure to require a minimum bid on it at the low end of the range to protect yourself.

GREAT EXPECTATIONS!

One other important point is that you must be sure to control the situation against exaggerated expectations. If you shoot for the moon, you may be disappointed when you don't get it. The same goes for your opponent. This is why it's important to keep your list of wants and needs in perspective. It would be wise to show your list to someone who has bought or sold something similar before. She or he can probably tell you if you are being realistic or just dreaming. After your negotiating experience grows, you will be able to judge for yourself, but until you achieve your black belt in bargaining, you should always seek help from those who have been there before.

Also, never assume that you're in a superior position. This would be like a large bully looking at the rather small Bruce Lee and assuming he is going to have an easy victim. What a mistake that would have been!

ANTICIPATE THE THREE POSSIBILITIES

To take advantage of an opponent's opening move, a smart martial artist must already have designed a response strategy. She will spend a part of every class practicing responses to every possible punch, kick, block, or throw until they become automatic.

By mentally preparing yourself for how you will respond to almost any situation, you give yourself a tremendous advantage over your competition. Sensei Tabuchi says that there are only three choices in the face of a challenge: the fighters can simply walk away, they can postpone the fight, or they can accept the challenge.

In negotiating, there are also three possibilities. If you are buying a product or service there are only three ways a seller can respond to your offer: First, the seller can accept it outright; second, the seller can counter the initial low offer with a higher price and/or different set of terms and conditions; third, the seller can simply reject it outright.

If the seller takes the deal as offered, you can move on to your next deal. If the seller comes back with a higher price, you must decide whether to accept that price or make a counter to the counterproposal. If the seller changes the terms and/or conditions, you must think about whether they are acceptable to you or if you want to counter this counterproposal. If the seller refuses to consider your offer at all, you have the choice to sweeten the deal, walk away, or come back later with a different offer. By the way, not knowing which response you will get is what makes negotiating fun and interesting.

If you are selling a product or service, there are only three ways you can respond to a buyer who offers less than your advertised price. You can accept the offer if you need the money badly enough. You can make a counterproposal to the buyer, which raises the price or changes the terms and conditions. Finally, you can simply counter the buyer back at full price, which is like saying "I won't negotiate."

By planning your response in advance, you are ready to get the best deal you can regardless of what happens because you have eliminated the element of surprise.

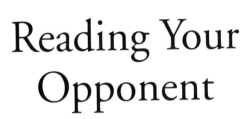

9

Reading Your Opponent

*Carefully, observe oneself and one's situation,
carefully observe others, and carefully observe one's environment.*

JIGORO KANO (FOUNDER OF JUDO)

Experienced martial artists know how to read their opponents almost as if they are able to read their minds. Once they are engaged, you can tell what style they practice and how to counter their moves. An observant fighter can also tell the state of mind and mood of the other person just by watching the person's breath, facial tenseness, and other cues.

The minute you enter the ring, you must be aware of your opponent. You start by analyzing his or her physical characteristics. Is the person tall or short, heavy or slim, and how long are his or her arms and legs? This gives you a sense of what the person will be capable of doing in the ring.

This kind of awareness is crucial to success and sometimes survival. It could let you win regardless of your opponent's strengths. However, you must choose the right technique for the right opponent. The same rules apply to negotiating.

OBSERVE CAREFULLY

Earlier I suggested that when bargaining, you be acutely aware of your opponent's posture, tone of voice, and other mannerisms, especially at the very beginning. By asking questions that you know the opponent is answering truthfully, you now have a baseline for how the person acts when he or she is telling the truth and not under stress. Anything that now deviates from the body language that you know is truthful is probably less than truthful. This has been proven through the science of kinesics, which is the study of nonverbal behaviors such as facial expressions and gestures. This science says you should watch out for the following:

INDICATORS OF TRUTH
- Head: tilted toward you
- Facial muscles: relaxed and fluid
- Hands: relaxed and palms open
- Voice: low and relaxed
- Rate of speech: slow and smooth
- Breathing: slow and even
- Eye pupils: wide
- Eye contact: direct and steady
- Posture: relaxed and stable
- Body: leaning forward
- Answers: complete
- Pauses: short, just for breath
- Verbal: normal

INDICATORS OF LYING
- Head: tilted away from you
- Facial muscles: tense and rigid
- Hands: tense and palms down
- Voice: higher and tense
- Rate of speech: quick and choppy
- Breathing: quick and uneven
- Eye pupils: narrow
- Eye contact: indirect and looking away
- Posture: tense and squirming
- Body: leaning away
- Answers: short
- Pauses: longer, thinking up answer
- Verbal: use of qualifies such as "basically," "generally," or "however."

Another dynamic you need to recognize is when other parties agree or disagree with you. The way to determine this is to make a statement you know they will absolutely disagree with and note their body language. For example, if you know the seller was not planning on including the speakers with the stereo you are purchasing, you might say, "If I recall correctly, your asking price included the speakers. Right?" Again, observe the body language compared to what you noticed before negotiations began. Black belt negotiators will even watch the pupils of the eyes of the other party as they discuss the terms. It's natural, when you hear or see something that you like, that your pupils will widen, and your pupils will narrow if it's something you don't like.

INDICATORS OF AGREEMENT
- Tilting the head toward you
- Putting a hand to the cheek
- Leaning forward
- Stroking the chin
- Laying pen or pencil down

INDICATORS OF DISAGREEMENT
- Head tilted away from you
- Furrowed brow
- Limited or no eye contact
- Tense cheek and neck muscles
- Crossed arms
- Shifting legs
- Stiff body

Speech can also signal patterns that indicate a person's state of mind. Does the person's language grow more emotive, more personal, which means he or she is being open with you? Sometimes speech becomes more rapid or slows down, which can indicate excitement or thoughtfulness, respectively.

A person's mood can also function as a prompt. If someone becomes more interested, it means you are on the right track. If someone becomes less interested, there is definitely something about your offer—or you—that the person doesn't like.

As you read or discuss the basic terms of your agreement out loud, look for any enthusiasm on your opponent's part. Note where the person becomes excited or more interested and where he or she shows little interest.

Studies show that women tend to be more observant than men, so men have to learn to watch for these kinds of physical cues very carefully. We all must pay attention, not just to individual gestures, but for patterns in gesture known as *clusters*, as grouped in the preceding lists. One gesture, taken out of context, could be misleading; however, certain combinations of gestures can be especially reliable indicators of a person's true feelings.

Although you should not infer truth, lying, agreement, or disagreement from any one gesture, when people are telling the truth, all their individual gestures, considered together, usually project a common, unified message. If they do not, this indicates incongruity, which generally implies that a person is lying or is uncomfortable. For example, when someone laughs nervously, the laugh and the nervousness are contradictory. A laugh generally indicates relaxation, but nervous body language is usually a sign that the person is uncomfortable.

DON'T ASSUME

Don't make assumptions about opponents from their manner, dress, speech, gender, or other outward appearance. In the dojo, when men spar with women, they may hold back a bit because, initially, they don't want to hurt them. Smart female fighters often use this to their advantage to score a few points early in the contest.

Grant Tabuchi is a very experienced businessman whose family has been in the United States for four generations. However, because he looks rather young and is Asian, many people assume he is not familiar with American contracts and finances. He related a story to me about when he was negotiating the ninth lease for his martial arts schools. He said, "The woman leasing agent assumed that I had no experience in commercial leases, so I just let her explain such clauses as 'triple net' and 'common area maintenance,' which gave *me* a chance to see what *she* knew. After she looked at my financial statement, however, it became clear to her that I was very experienced at leasing commercial properties and her whole attitude towards me changed. Suddenly we became equals, but in the process she gave me a lot of information she might not have otherwise provided."

Women can do the same if others assume they cannot negotiate. Just let them continue to assume until you have gained as much information as you can and then turn it against them, as Sensei Tabuchi did.

My real estate partner, Stuart, has a speech impediment; he talks a lot like Elmer Fudd on the Bugs Bunny cartoons ("Cwazy wabbit!"). Even though he has one of the most brilliant mathematical minds I've ever encountered, many people assume he isn't very smart because of the way he talks. When we would make an offer to purchase a house, the sellers and their agents would usually slowly explain to us why they needed a higher price and all the needs the seller had to meet to make the deal work for him. While they were carefully making sure that my partner understood everything, Stu would be furiously calculating things in his mind, like this: "If the seller carried back a second loan at a favorable below-market rate, we could increase our offering price and actually have lower payments than with our previous offer" or "If we raised the price but had the seller give us a credit back for painting and repairs, we would actually save money because we would add the additional money to our loan at a much lower interest rate than charging the repairs on high-interest-rate credit cards." The sellers were usually so taken aback by the fact that they were getting what they wanted and awed by the complexity of the way Stu put it together that they routinely just accepted it without question. We used people's prejudices against them to put together deals like these to obtain tens of thousands of dollars of savings because the other parties didn't realize they were being outsmarted until it was too late.

If, at the bargaining table, you prejudge your opposition by physical characteristics, gender, race, or any other outward characteristic, you won't be able to read your opponent accurately and thus will not choose the correct technique as a countermove. Once people respond to an initial offer, you can begin to gauge their true position.

Be careful, because even the most experienced martial artist has been fooled. Fighters have been known to stand close, only to make their opponents believe they are more confident than they really are. Don't let this happen to you. Empty your mind before sitting down at the bargaining table. Assume that everyone is your equal regardless of first impressions.

WHAT STYLE DO THEY PRACTICE?

Different martial artists practice different styles, from tae kwon do to aikido to judo to tai chi, and many more. From the moment they take a stance, you can tell what style they practice, and you would respond to them accordingly.

In the same way, there are different personality styles to be dealt with in negotiations. There are some people who attempt to lead you to accept their deal by being controlling and assertive. Others attempt to persuade you to give them what they want by being sociable and friendly. Then there are those who appeal to your emotions to bring about a deal. Finally, there are bargainers who try to convince you to see their side through the use of logic and by providing reams of data to prove their point.

In 1928, a psychologist named William Moulton Marston developed personality testing and assessments that classify people's personalities into four aspects by testing their preferences in word associations. These have become known as the DISC personality styles, based on these four aspects of personality:

1. *Dominant:* relating to control, power, and assertiveness
2. *Influential:* relating to social situation and communications
3. *Steady:* relating to patience, persistence, and thoughtfulness
4. *Conscientious:* relating to structure and organization

Believe it or not, different styles of martial arts attract people with different personality styles. There are hard martial arts like tae kwon do and soft ones like tai chi, and the speed, discipline, and use of power attract people with similar personalities to the same styles. Here's my analysis of how the DISC personality types are related to martial arts styles.

Dominant personalities tend to be direct, demanding, and decisive and often practice tae kwon do, which is a martial art from Korea. It is known as "the way of the foot and the fist" because it is characterized by fast, high, spinning kicks and a system of hand strikes. It is a hard offensive and defensive martial art, using tension in the muscles and a very direct approach, which is why so many D's are drawn to it.

To be successful when negotiating with a Dominant, you should first build respect, but then get to the point quickly. Talk about the value of the deal by focusing on facts of the deal, not the people involved. Dominants experience the biggest challenge negotiating with Steady types because S's are all about feelings and D's just want to get to the bottom line. D's must learn to get in touch with their emotions and not only share a bit of how they're feeling but inquire about how the S's feel about the deal as well.

Influential personalities are usually social, persuasive, and friendly and are very often found practicing aikido, which is a Japanese martial art known as "the way of the harmonious spirit." It uses principles of energy and motion to redirect, neutralize, and control attackers wrapped in a spiritual cocoon. When bargaining with I's, try to be friendly and listen carefully to their wants and needs. Focus more on the big picture in general terms and not the details of the deal. Influentials have the most difficulty communicating with the Conscientious, since C's want lots of detail, whereas I's are not detail-oriented. I's must make an effort to gather as many statistics and facts as possible before, during, or after the negotiations.

Steady personalities usually like stability and are peace seeking; they are often drawn to judo, which is a Japanese martial art referred to as the "gentle way." It is strictly a defensive style that applies the principle of leverage to use an opponent's own momentum to throw him to the ground. If you find yourself in negotiations with Steady personalities, you'll be most effective by taking an interest in them as people and giving them time to adjust to change. Clearly define the goals of the deal and talk about how the person feels about the terms and conditions as well as sharing your own state of emotions. Steady personalities have the biggest challenge negotiating with Dominants because, although the S's want to share feelings, the D's don't want any part of it. Steady personalities must minimize any talk about feelings and get down to business as quickly as possible. If you feel like you're being run over by a Mack truck, you can say to the D, "I feel you're not listening to me . . ." Even the most hardened D will take this as a sign to slow down.

Conscientious personalities tend to be slow, critical thinkers and sometimes are even perfectionists. Many of these people like the discipline found in tai chi, which is a Chinese martial art also known as "the hardness that dwells within softness." It's called a soft style because its practitioners develop the ability to use strong energy from the mind and body, without any unnecessary stress or tension. Movements are executed very precisely, slowly, and deliberately so the form can be appreciated. When dealing with Conscientious people, you should definitely avoid surprises by being very prepared and explaining the deal in a logical, accurate, and clear manner. Back up what you say with as many statistics and facts as you can gather. Conscientious personalities find it most difficult to relate to Influentials, since C's want facts and figures but I's prefer generalities. To bridge this gulf, C's must provide the overall goal of the negotiations first, and then reinforce it with details.

Which DISC Personality Style Are You?

The first step in using the DISC system is to identify your own personality style. Take this short quiz and find out which you are, and then begin to analyze which style your bargaining opponents are.

1. For each set of four adjectives *across*, rank each adjective on the basis of how well it describes you. Put a 7 in the brackets next to the adjective that best describes you, a 5 for the next closest adjective, a 3 for the next, and a 1 for the least descriptive of you. Each line across should have a 7, 5, 3, and 1; no ties are allowed.

COLUMN 1	COLUMN 2	COLUMN 3	COLUMN 4
Decisive ( )	Outgoing ( )	Sensitive ( )	Analytical ( )
Competitive ( )	Obliging ( )	Playful ( )	Obedient ( )
Adventurous ( )	Life of Party ( )	Moderate ( )	Precise ( )
Determined ( )	Convincing ( )	Good natured ( )	Careful ( )
Forceful ( )	Optimistic ( )	Lenient ( )	Accurate ( )
Stubborn ( )	Persuasive ( )	Gentle ( )	Humble ( )
TOTAL ( )	TOTAL ( )	TOTAL ( )	TOTAL ( )

2. Add your scores down each column and put the total in the bottom box. Make sure the grand total of all columns equals 96 to test that you added correctly. The column with the highest total number reflects your strongest personality trait.

3. Interpretation
   _____ Column 1—Dominant
   _____ Column 2—Influential
   _____ Column 3—Steady
   _____ Column 4—Conscientious

(Courtesy of Tina Ramirez—DISC expert)

There is no one best personality type. In fact, we are all a combination of personalities, but the DISC system shows your prevalent style and it can help you understand your opponents and relate to them more effectively.

IDENTIFY PHYSICAL PATTERNS

We all have behavior patterns. For instance, a fighter might regularly make two jabs and then punch over and over, doing the same set of moves. Obviously, knowing this can be very helpful to an opponent who, recognizing the pattern, will be ready to block the punch and then counter with a kick.

At the bargaining table, try to identify any habits in your opponent's body language that might signal the beginning or end of a pattern. The beginning signals that a set of moves is coming that you should be familiar with and know how to counter. The end signals that you're entering the unknown and you need to be ready for anything. For example, if an opponent always raises a hand to touch his or her temple just before asking for a concession, whenever you see this you should have a counterproposal ready.

Obviously, you do not want to fall prey to this fault yourself. Try to break up your tactics to be unpredictable. You might mirror your opponent for a while and then do the opposite for a time. This will certainly catch the other person off guard.

OBSERVING YOUR RANGE

In a martial arts tournament, you should watch not only your opponent's physical actions and demeanor but how far apart you are. Range is the distance at which two fighters can contact each other. Until they reach this point, the contest has not really begun. Beyond this distance, you cannot score nor can you be scored against. Observing the range tells you the opportunities and dangers you are facing. Sensei Tabuchi says that there are three fighting ranges, which he calls *circles*:

Circle Three: This is the farthest fighting range, where our feet cannot touch, even when the legs are fully extended. This also means our fists can't reach each other. Although this is the safe zone, you cannot score any points from here, either.

In negotiating, you start outside the fighting range but should move quickly into closer quarters, or you can never reach agreement. This is the psychological and emotional distance at which you begin your negotiations, but your rapport building should begin to draw the other party toward you. At this distance, you are not yet homing in on any target. The principal task is to build rapport because this sets the foundation upon which the rest of the talks will rest. You will put out feelers, but they are not meant to force a decision or a commitment to the deal itself. The goal is, first, to see if your objectives are even in the same ballpark and, second to gauge whether this is a person you want to do business with. Is the person civilized, reasonable, and fair? Sometimes the deal is beside the point. Your sanity is more important than whatever you're bargaining for.

Circle Two: This is where fighters' feet can touch but not the arms. This is when you use long-range techniques, which would include kicks and feints, to draw your opponent closer. Taller fighters tend to prefer this range so they can take advantage of their longer legs. Shorter fighters can only block, so they must try to get closer to score.

In negotiating, you're making a subtle shift in focus from the individual to the deal. This is where the bargaining begins, but the parties are still far apart. You throw out *feelers* to see how receptive the other party is by saying something like "Would you pay full price for the guitar if I throw in some free lessons?" In this circle you begin to make vague offers and even vaguer counteroffers to see how close or far apart you are.

Circle One: This circle is very close quarters where the hands can contact but the distance make kicks impossible. Shorter fighters tend to prefer this range for obvious reasons. In negotiations, this is where the details are worked out and agreements are reached.

Range in negotiating is not only the emotional gap between the two parties but also the distance between where you are currently and what you want to be. Both parties must be close enough in their needs and demands to come to agreement. However, the closer you come to an agreement, the more alert you must be, because when you are this close, small mistakes can cost you dearly. Unfortunately, most novice negotiators tend to let down their guard just as the deal is being finalized. This is the absolute opposite of what they should be doing.

It's important not to be too anxious to get within fighting distance, or you could fall into a trap. You should do what we call "ease into distance." The trick martial artists use is that, instead of moving their feet, they simply shuffle them or lean toward their opponent, which moves them more subtly within range. You can do this in negotiating by observing how much the other party gives in each time. If, all of a sudden, the other party makes a big drop in price or asks you for a large concession, that is the time to be wary. Your range just got a lot closer for no apparent reason. This is the time to recheck all your figures to make sure the other party hasn't sneaked something past you.

In negotiations, you can make small concessions on unimportant issues to see if you can draw the other side in toward you. If you do, then begin in earnest. If not, you may decide that doing a deal with this party is not worth it at this time.

Martial artists are always aware of their range because just a fraction of an inch can make the difference between winning and losing. It's the difference between a hit and a miss.

When bargaining, you must also be constantly aware of your range. You should always be moving closer to an agreement, or there is something wrong.

Sometimes the only way to learn your opponent's range is to test the person. Experienced martial artists may even let opponents hit them in a nonvital area like the shoulder. This tells you a lot about the opponent but reveals nothing about you. In negotiating, you can do this by finding the other person's *walkaway point*.

THE WALKAWAY POINT

The most important question to ask before starting any negotiation is "Is it worth the investment of my time to start the bargaining process?" You may decide that the time you will have to spend far outweighs the small amount you might save. Sometimes, after you assess a situation, you may decide that a confrontation is just not worth it. I've seen drivers get into a physical altercation over a parking spot! This is what can happen when two parties harden their positions. Is it really worth fighting over? All one person has to do is drive away, and that person is likely to find another spot even closer.

Likewise, you may decide that the effort is not worth it and walk away from a negotiation. There's no more powerful position in bargaining than being able to walk away.

Sensei Tabuchi says, "It's important in combative situations on the street to decide early if you are going to engage your opponent or walk away. After that you are too involved mentally and physically."

In negotiations, you should decide immediately after the first response whether to walk away or continue, for exactly the same reason. If it looks like you're just too far apart, it might be better to leave the other person with his or her dignity, so the person might be willing to come back later with a better offer.

If you are a seller and there are many potential buyers available and one offer is very low, it might be best for all concerned to dismiss it out of hand. If the buyer really needs what you have, he or she will surely return with a more serious offer. If you are a buyer and there is only one store that carries what you want, you are not in a very strong bargaining positioning. Perhaps you should wait for a sale?

In addition, being willing to walk away puts the other person's offer to the ultimate test. Was the person serious or just "fishing"?

As discussions progress, try to find the other party's walkaway point. This is where they will not bargain any further but will walk out. We Americans like to call this the *bottom line*. Recognize that when someone says, "This is my bottom line," this is most likely not it. When the person actually starts to walk away, that's the person's bottom line. Once you know the person's walkaway point, you can choose your countering tactics.

You must also decide upon your own walkaway point. What's the minimum deal you are willing to accept? Then you must stick to it. Black belts are disciplined. Without discipline, you might end up with *gamblers' syndrome*. When undisciplined gamblers start losing, they keep playing, hoping to recover their money, but all they do is keep digging themselves a deeper hole. Professional gamblers have a set amount they decide they can afford to lose, and when they reach it they walk away from the table without hesitation.

For martial artists as well as negotiators, the most effective tactic can be to withdraw from a no-win contest before it even gets started. If you are challenged by an opponent and you just don't feel like it's worth a fight, or perhaps it's a battle you don't believe you can win, you can simply refuse the encounter. The other party will view this in one of two ways: (1) They may assume that you are afraid of them, or (2) they may think they are not enough of a challenge to bother with. The only difference is in how you tell them "no." If you say it with a straight face, they'll assume the former, but if you say it with a smile on your face, they'll assume the latter.

GREEN BELT TEST

The next time you are shopping at the mall or any fancy store, pick some item that you've always wanted but never seriously considered buying, such as a Persian carpet, 3-carat diamond ring, quadraphonic stereo system, Rolex watch, or other luxury item, and ask the salesperson to show it to you. Then ask the following questions:

1. How long have you been working here?
2. Do you have one of these yourself?
3. How do you know so much about this?
4. How long has this been in the store?
5. What's the best way to care for it?
6. What extras does it come with (warranty, maintenance plan, etc.)?
7. What would be the total cost (including shipping, installation, etc.)?
8. How much do you think the owner would take for this?

Once you have finished, sit down and answer the following questions:

1. What was the salesperson's fighting stance (open or closed)?
2. Did you feel comfortable with the salesperson?
3. Was your body language open or closed to the salesperson?
4. Did the salesperson mirror you?
5. Did the salesperson ask you rapport-building questions?
6. Were you calm or nervous?
7. What was the salesperson's response to the question "How much do you think the owner would take for this?"
8. Did you notice the salesperson's truthful state?
9. Did you notice any indicators of lying?
10. What principles from the previous chapters in this section applied to this exercise?

If you were not completely comfortable asking investigative questions and using this rapport-building process, keep doing it until it becomes second nature.

PART IV

Blue Belt

The plant reaches for the sky toward new heights.

At this level, students often spar with people above their own level, so they can see how much more there is yet to learn. In doing so, they pick up more advanced tactics from superior fighters.

In Chapter 10—"Countering Your Opponent's Moves"—the negotiator will be receiving his first offer from the opponent, which is like a fighter receiving his first punch. He has to know instinctively how to respond. The Blue Belt learns specific tactics for use in the ring that can throw the opponent off and put the reader on the best possible footing.

Chapter 11—"Finding Middle Ground"—continues this learning process. The middle ground in a negotiation corresponds to the place on the mat where fighters in a martial arts contest are willing to give and take blows—it's where the bargaining really begins. The reader will find a place of agreement to build on. He has already tested his opponent and knows it is worth it to continue bargaining. Just as the fighter does, the Blue Belt negotiator must reach down and find resilience within himself, find the energy to handle the emotional stress.

This leads directly to Chapter 12—"Distancing Yourself From the Battle." Martial arts students are often defeated by their own emotions. When they are kicked or punched over and over, and cannot get in a hit of their own, frustration mounts. At the bargaining table, it's the same feeling when the other party seems to be getting all his wants and needs fulfilled, and we are getting nothing. At the Blue Belt stage, readers understand that if they give into their emotions, they lose. That is why this chapter teaches readers how to become emotionally detached and illustrates why it is so important.

10

Countering Your Opponent's Moves

*When confronting an imcoming attack, the attack is parried
or deflected and a counterattack is delivered at the same time.*

BRUCE LEE

During the first minute or so of any contest, martial artists warm up by sparring and jabbing just to test each other. When an opponent makes a move like a punch or a kick, it gives you the opportunity to respond with a block, throw, or strike of your own. However, you don't want to reveal too much about your strengths and especially your weaknesses at this early stage. Most savvy fighters just counter with a move similar to what their opponent just made, so they don't overcommit.

In negotiating, how you respond to the first offer is critical. The best course of action is to be noncommittal, because that lets you test your opponent without giving away your position. By not turning your cards over on the table, it encourages the other party to turn a few cards over to keep the game going.

How can you make a move, yet still be noncommittal? Whether you're buying or selling, simply say something that doesn't tip your hand. At the same time, you have to let the other party know that his or her initial offer is unacceptable. As many savvy salespeople know, the best way to control a conversation is by asking questions. Whether you're the buyer or the seller, you might say, "How did you come up with that amount?" or "Why do you want me to do that?" Another noncommittal response is known in negotiating terms as *the vise*—a statement that forces the other person to make a move.

All you say is, "You'll have to do better than that," which throws the ball back to the other party and demands that the person make an improved offer.

Once you say that, just be silent and wait for the response. Then listen when it comes. Many novice negotiators wrongly believe that to make another person agree to the deal, they must *talk* them into it. What they usually end up doing is talking *themselves out* of a deal instead. The more they talk, the greater the chances they'll say something that hurts their position. Saying too much gives you the opportunity to say the wrong thing.

People also believe that to control a conversation, they must talk continuously. In reality, the person who asks questions is in control because the responding party must first stop and gather his or her thoughts, and then answer the question that was asked. The person asking questions is the one doing the prompting and setting the stage. Where the questioner leads, the answerer must follow.

Martial artists always choose which technique they will use to respond based on the initial moves of their opponents. When the opposing party comes out hard and aggressive, for instance, it's usually best to be evasive until the person tires out. If an opponent is hesitant and tentative, the fighter will probably want to take a harder approach than if he or she is faced with someone who is more intense and direct.

You have the same choices in negotiations. If you are a seller and the buyer's first offer is completely one-sided in his or her own favor, you can simply reject the offer or counter the offer at full price. What you're doing is making the decision not to negotiate at this time. Let's say you're in a clothing store looking at a suit. You ask the salesperson, "What's the best price you could give me on this?" and the person simply repeats the sticker price. This indicates that the store is firm in its price at the moment. Telling you the sticker price is the same as saying, "I won't negotiate." You can either wait for the suit to go on sale, talk to the manager, or take your business somewhere else.

Sometimes after sizing up your opponent, you should be aggressive and take advantage of obvious opportunities. In sparring, martial artists know they have an advantage when their opponent's weight is on their back foot, which makes the person slow to respond. You would punch or kick immediately before the opponent has a chance to react.

The approach you take in negotiating varies, depending on the circumstances. It's the day before Christmas and every parent in the tristate area is trying to buy PlayStation 3. Your kid's heart is set on it, and from the front of the store you spot the last box. You rush toward it just as another father is trying to beat you to the goal. If you've been to this store a dozen times and you know a shortcut, you have every right to take it. Or, if the other father does get there first, you can offer him a $50 bill to let you buy it. The outcome all depends on who wants it the most and who is the most aggressive.

TACTICS: WAYS TO RESPOND TO OPENING MOVES

In martial arts, a point of resistance is anyplace where people refuse to give ground. If you encounter resistance in the opening moves, you should not meet it head-on but, instead, step around it or even go with it. Instead of having the other person's energy focused directly against you, turn it around and use it against that person. Not only do you avoid being hit, but you can score points by using the opponent's own momentum to throw him or her to the ground. When judo masters feel resistance, they simply redirect their opponents' energy in any direction they wish.

There are five specific tactics you can use to respond to an opening move at the bargaining table. They will help you obtain the most beneficial outcome for your side.

1. Using Resistance

In martial arts contests, when you encounter strong resistance it usually means your opponents feel they are backed into a corner. They may feel they have retreated as much as they are willing and have now decided to take a stand. When you realize this, you can take advantage of the situation by not pushing them back any farther, because people will fight ferociously when they are cornered. Instead, savvy fighters will take some of the pressure off by giving opponents room to breathe.

In negotiating, people tend to resist the most whenever they are emotionally involved and wherever their needs are invested. The resistance indicates that this is something they want and possibly need. You can use the energy of their own desire in your favor. The goal is to find out what that attachment is, because this becomes a vital striking point for you. It is the one place you know you have leverage. Empathize with their emotions by listening and then saying something back that shows you heard them. Or you can also encourage them to tell you more about this possession and what it means to them. One extra benefit is that as long as they are focused on this, they are more likely to give in on other issues.

2. Feinting

In martial arts, *feinting* refers to pretending to aim at a part of the body you're really not interested in striking, which distracts your opponent from the part you *are* interested in hitting. It's like a magician who shows you with a flourish that there is nothing up his right sleeve to distract you from the rabbit he is pulling out of the left.

Early in my martial arts training I was taught to feint by moving my head forward as if I was going to advance and then suddenly stepping back to kick. I also learned to pretend to sweep an opponent's leg with my foot but stop halfway into my move, then step forward on that foot and punch instead. Another move was to jerk a knee up quickly as if I was going to kick an opponent just to see what the reaction would be. Armed with this knowledge, I was ready to respond in a way the opponent wasn't expecting.

In negotiating, it is vital never to go after your primary target first. If you do, the other party will know that this is important to you and make you pay dearly to get it. To try to pretend later that you really weren't interested in it, after you've already tipped your hand, will be useless. The other party already knows your target—and your weakness.

When my wife and I walk into a leather shop, she usually makes a beeline for the perfect handbag to complement her latest outfit. The problem with this habit is that the salesperson now knows she really wants it and will put pressure on me to buy it for her at full price. So I am training her to mentally select what she wants, then talk to the clerk about a *different* purse. We find out how negotiable that bag is, then we walk out and go to another store. Armed with our previous experience, we will come back a bit later and begin bargaining on the purse my wife really wants, almost as if it was an afterthought. We will usually get a much better deal than was previously offered because the salesperson knows we were willing to walk away before and will probably do it again if we don't get a great deal this time.

3. Flinching

In martial arts we will sometimes grimace and pretend that an opponent's blow hurts us more than it really does, just to make the person think we're inept or scared. This pulls the opponent toward us in the false belief that he or she can now get in an easy shot. Now, as the opponent comes forward, we are ready to counter the attack and mount one of our own. Flinching means to mislead another person with a contrived physical expression.

In negotiating, you flinch for the opposite reason. You're not trying to mislead; you're doing it to visibly show what you're *really* thinking when someone presents an offer. This puts the person on the right track straightaway, so he or she doesn't think the offer is in any way acceptable. White belt bargainers tend not to flinch because they want to be nice. They don't want to make a nasty face and be thought of as disagreeable, so, instead, they just sit there stoically, even when they're totally dumbfounded by a ridiculous offer. Of course, this sends the whole proceeding off in the wrong direction, leading the offerer to believe that the other party is seriously considering the deal. Flinching gives someone a physical sign that the offer is unacceptable, sending a clear message that he or she must sweeten the deal now or you will walk away.

There are thousands of ways to flinch. You can laugh out loud at the offer or just wipe your brow with your hand while loudly exhaling. Your opponent will get the point.

The key to making your flinch truly effective is that after you respond, you must shut up. The silence has more of an effect than if you start talking because it creates a vacuum in the conversation that the other party will feel obligated to fill. Be absolutely silent and wait for the other party to respond to your flinch. Generally, Americans, Brits, and others are not used to observing silence during a conversation. This tends to be one of the most uncomfortable parts of negotiations for them. If silence makes you nervous, the key is not to stare at your opponent; look at your notes or stay busy with some other distraction as if you're not interested in the response and are thinking about walking away from the whole thing. Again, the problem with *not* flinching and being noncommittal is that it implies to the other party that you are seriously considering the offer, which at best tells the person he or she has the upper hand and at worst wastes everyone's time by proceeding in the wrong direction.

How do you know if your flinch has been effective? A great flinch makes the other party actually feel guilty or ridiculous to have made such an inappropriate offer *and* causes them to raise the offer. For example, I was trying to sell my two-year-old Alfa Romeo sports car for $25,000 to a young man who seemed to really like it. After the test drive he said, "I'll give you fifteen thousand for it." I just laughed, shook my head, and stroked the lustrous finish of the car without saying a word. He stammered, "Uh, how about eighteen thousand?" In response, I just reached out my hands as if to grab the keys from him, and he quickly said, "Okay, twenty two thousand." Eventually we settled on $24,500, which was $1,000 more than I had expected to get. Just these two flinches (the laugh and reaching for the keys) got him to increase his offer by $7,000, and in return I gave him nothing but a couple of flinches. This is the power of the flinch.

Flinching doesn't come naturally to most people, so you must practice this tactic in a mirror until you become really convincing. When actor Jim Carrey was young, he used to practice making funny expressions in the mirror, just to see how elastic he could make his face. Needless to say, it paid off big-time. Practicing can work for you, too. It is essential to becoming a black belt negotiator.

However, you must learn to vary your flinches. If you make the same squeamish face every time an offer doesn't meet your expectations, it will become obvious that you're using it as a ploy. Try on different faces and reactions until you know that each one is believable.

Here are a few simple flinches you can start with:

- Just repeat the person's offer in a loud, questioning voice. For example, yell, *"Ninety-nine dollars?"* That's all you need to say. Leave the rest to the person's imagination.
- Simply laugh and then say, "Seriously, what were you *really* thinking about paying?"
- Put your hand over your face as if the offer has just given you a headache, and shake your head side to side as if you're saying no.
- Jerk back in your chair as if you have been given an electric shock.
- Let all of the air loudly out of your lungs as if you've been punched in the stomach.
- Suck your next breath in through your teeth like someone who's just stepped into a buck of ice water.

Remember, if you respond to an offer with a believable flinch and then shut up, the buyer will probably raise the offer, or sellers will likely lower their price without you having given them anything more than a flinch. It can't get any cheaper than that.

4. Rejecting the First Offer

When someone makes you an offer, it is crucial that you *never accept the first one.* Now, this advice usually scares most beginners because they are afraid the other person might change his or her mind. This is a valid concern because even a small counterproposal to an offer gives your opponent the chance to back out of the deal. However, if someone does walk after such a minor provocation, it means the person wasn't serious anyway, and the negotiations would probably have never have gone through.

It's ironic that what actually happens is the opposite. If you accept the first offer with no counterproposal, there's a better chance that the other person will *now* back out of the deal. Why? By immediately accepting the deal, you send a signal that the other party could have done better. Otherwise, why would you grab at it so eagerly? As a result, the person may immediately have second thoughts and want to cancel the agreement. He or she will either come back later with a more favorable offer or take the deal somewhere else. Also, by accepting the offer as is, you could raise the other party's suspicions that something is fishy and you're trying to move in for the kill and get it over with quickly. The person might imagine that the product is defective, that you can't be trusted, that you don't intend to deliver what you promised, or that there is some other reason you would jump at the offer without changing it at all. These concerns could easily cause the person to rescind the agreement. It's the same uneasy feeling you get when some shady character offers you a Rolex watch for $100 in Times Square. More likely than not, it's not even a Timex, much less a Rolex.

The exception to this principle would perhaps occur when you know you are dealing with an unsophisticated negotiator. You probably won't have to bother with a counteroffer at all because it is likely that the person will just pay full price without question. In this case, take the person's money and then sell him or her every option and add-on you've got. The profit from this one sale will give you more flexibility in handling veteran hagglers.

Even if the offer is very close or even exactly what you want, you still want to make a small counteroffer for all of the aforementioned reasons. This may not even involve money. If you're selling a house, ask the buyer to close escrow a week sooner, or use a different title company. If you're selling a laptop computer, explain that at this price the carrying case and extra battery can't be included. Just find something about the deal to change.

Italians are some of the best negotiators in the world. When I was bargaining for a crystal chandelier in Murano, Italy, it took me two hours to convince the store to drop its price some $20,000. We were both at the top of our game and the bartering would have gone on even longer, but the manager finally said he would accept my price as long as I was willing to pay for shipping back to the United States, which he could no longer afford to do. That was the point at which I knew I had reached his bottom line. I accepted. When negotiating, don't beat a dead horse. When it's done, it's done.

Although it is true that the Italian manager and I were both professional negotiators, I had the confidence to reject his initial offer of a $5,000 discount off the retail price, even though my wife and I really wanted that chandelier. This is a tactic you can easily practice, too. There really is nothing to be afraid of. If someone is going to back out because of a small counteroffer, what do you think will happen when bigger issues arise? If the person is going to back out, give him or her the chance to do it early so you'll have the time to find a more serious buyer or seller.

Remember, most people take acceptance of the first offer to mean that they must have made a mistake and could have done better. To them, that's the only reason you would have accepted it without a fight. Bargaining is expected, and not doing it just seems fishy.

5. Recognizing That Everyone Has a Predetermined Position

Sometimes sellers have psychological blocks to assessing accurately what their goods are really worth, and buyers have arbitrary limits on what they will pay. If it becomes obvious that this is what you are facing, especially early in the negotiations, you just may want to walk away until the passage of time makes the other party more realistic and, therefore, cooperative.

Recognize that everyone has some kind of predetermined position and it does not have to be based anywhere in logic. I met a house seller to whom I had proven that properties comparable to his were selling for $400,000, yet he insisted that his was worth $500,000. When I asked why he felt his house was worth $100,000 more than similar homes in the area he replied, "I have all oak baseboards in my home." Almost any real estate professional anywhere will tell you that an amenity like this adds absolutely nothing to the value of a home except perhaps to help it sell a bit faster than its competition. So I refused to take his listing at this price, but another broker did. It sat on the market for over nine months and eventually sold for $380,000. The only thing that made this seller realistic about his original position was learning the hard way over time.

Don't laugh and don't be upset when the other party has unrealistic expectations. If they are not brought back to reality by showing data that backs up your position, it may be time to simply walk away. It certainly could take time for them to be convinced that they need to readjust their thinking. For instance, in 2006 home prices in the United States stopped increasing after an unprecedented nine-year rise, and in some areas prices even retreated to a certain extent. It took over a year for most home sellers to get used to the idea that they didn't live in the Land of Oz, and prices would not keep rising forever. Some people just refuse to recognize reality when they see it.

MAKE SURE YOUR NEEDS ARE MET

The main goal at this stage of the contest is to be sure your needs are met. If not, you might as well walk away now and save everyone a lot of wasted time. As we've seen, needs are pretty straightforward. They are the bare minimum you must get in order to be satisfied with the deal.

If you are buying a new desktop computer, you might need a 17-inch monitor, Windows Vista software, and a 250-gigabyte hard drive for under $500. It would be nice to have a 19-inch monitor, a scanner, and a printer within your budget, but that depends on your negotiating skills. However, if a computer doesn't meet your minimum needs, you won't even bother looking at it.

This is where having clear needs and wants lists comes in handy. As you go through the negotiation, just tick off your needs as they are met.

11

Finding Middle Ground

The middle ground is the most crucial in martial arts and negotiating.
MICHAEL SOON LEE

In any martial arts contest, you are always looking for a comfortable spot from which to execute most of your favorite moves. In this middle ground, fighters give and take blows, scoring as much as they can while giving up as few points as possible.

The middle ground in a negotiation is where the real bargaining begins. This stage is characterized by the need to find common ground so the process can move forward. Both parties are throwing their wants onto the table to find out where they converge—each place of agreement representing one more problem that can be set aside, thus shortening the list you have to get through before an agreement can be reached. The focus soon becomes narrowed to the few areas of discord. This whole process builds confidence because both parties can see that momentum is building.

Once you reach this point, you have already done your homework about your opponent and the entire subject of the negotiation. You have mentally warmed up and spent sufficient time building rapport. By previously testing your opponent, you found out what he or she can and cannot do to close this deal. You also determined that your needs could be met, so you know this is not just a fishing expedition. You are a serious contender.

This stage of the negotiation is often more stressful and emotionally draining than anything that went on earlier. Now you know that this deal could work for you, so you're much more emotionally attached than you were in the previous stage, where you always had one foot out the door.

By now you should also have gained a pretty good sense of your opponent's personality style, any predictable tendencies, temperament, and a little about the person's background and experience, which gives you a level of comfort. But you weren't scoring any big points in the negotiation. Now you'll want to score as many as possible by adding some of your wants to the deal, yet not lose the essential elements—your needs. At this point, you should still have a fair amount of energy, unless the first stage was particularly troublesome.

However, you may find that the picture doesn't look so rosy. You might realize that you are in trouble. Perhaps you overreached with your offers and asked for too much. Perhaps you've gone so far as to offend the other party, and it looks like the person is about to walk away. Or you might realize that you've overestimated your opponent's strength and have been too generous. You may be considering the prospect of withdrawing your offer and starting again later, but you realize that even that could backfire. The other party is not likely to forget the largesse of your previous offer and let you backpedal.

After the initial talks, it's also possible that you recognize that you're over-matched by a much stronger opponent. This is a good time to consider walking away before investing any more time in the transaction. Otherwise, you need to go into a defensive mode.

Much of the time, however, you will be feeling optimistic about the deal, since you should have systematically gotten your needs met. And yet you may be uneasy for another reason: Now you might actually have to make a commitment. "Do I really want to go through with this deal?" is a common source of anxiety.

This is, indeed, a time of mixed emotions. When you can see that the end is in sight, there is a tendency to rush toward it, and in your hurry you might disregard some of your wants just to get the haggling over with. Don't do it. This can be the most fruitful part of the negotiations, if you are patient.

This critical part of the negotiation takes a great deal of skill to handle. It separates good negotiators from great ones.

ADJUST YOUR FOCUS FROM NEEDS TO WANTS

If you are going to win a martial arts contest, you must shift your focus from being defensive and merely testing your opponent to really trying to score points. This means that for every point your opponent scores, you score two. Most martial artists are thinking, "I survived the first few jabs, so now let's see how good my training really is." There is a definite increase in aggression and competitiveness.

As we said previously, a negotiator's focus changes from needs to wants. At this point, you should have met your needs, checking them off your list. Otherwise, there's really not much point in continuing the discussion. Now it's time to really concentrate on winning the match, which, in negotiating, means getting as many of your wants as you can in exchange for giving up as little as possible.

Needs are very clear-cut, and you know you'll walk away if these aren't satisfied. There is no hemming and hawing, no "Will I?" or "Won't I?" Needs are driven by rational factors such as price, product specifications, product performance, and other clear metrics.

The challenge is that your wants are not usually so clear. They make the deal better for you, but you might be willing to forgo any or all of them, depending on other factors.

It's harder to determine crucial wants than critical needs because they can seem so similar. People will readily tell you their needs because needs are black-and-white. They are concrete. You absolutely know you have to have them. Wants, conversely, are harder to categorize and can be emotionally charged. They are not a given at all. Perhaps certain ones should be part of the package, but if they aren't, do you really want to give up the whole package? Needs involve logic, but wants satisfy an emotional voice. Few people *need* chocolate chip cookies when they're deciding whether to buy a food basket, but plenty of people will swear they can't live without them. If you run into a want such as this, you might as well consider it a need.

If you recall Maslow's Hierarchy of Needs from high school, you will remember that the most basic needs are physical—like food and water. Above the physical level is the need for safety, which is security of employment and resources. The third level of need is love and belonging, including friendship and having a family. The fourth level is status, which means being respected and recognized by others. The fifth and highest level is self-actualization, which is an appreciation of life and the desire to fulfill your own potential.

The higher you go up the Hierarchy of Needs, the less tangible and the more ethereal they are. You can easily tell when you've had enough food and water, but how much self-actualization is enough? It's strictly up to each individual to decide, and that is what makes this stage of the proceedings so challenging.

In negotiating, whatever the opponents ask for, it is important that you ask for something of roughly the same value. If they are asking for a large concession, you should as well. If they ask for something rather small, then yours should be relatively minor as well. Here's why: If they ask for something large and you ask for something small in return, they'll think something is fishy. If they ask for a small concession and you request something comparatively large, they'll think you're greedy. Either way, it's an imbalance, and this will not provide a very solid foundation for a positive relationship.

MONEY IS NOT ALWAYS THE MOST IMPORTANT ISSUE

Sensei Tabuchi says that the middle of the martial arts contest is where you should perform your fanciest moves, loudest yells, and most difficult techniques to accumulate the most points during the round. In a negotiation, it is also the stage where you try to be as creative as possible. Earlier in the proceedings, discussions over money tend to be fairly logical. Amounts of money go up and down, and that's about it. Other issues are not quite so linear. If you are bartering with a collector who wants your doll collection in exchange for his baseball card collection, and you've had one of those dolls since childhood and don't want to give it up, and he has an original Mickey Mantle card that his father gave him, whose collection is really worth the most? How do you work out the details when the value isn't so easy to measure?

When you reach this point in negotiations, you really have to pull away from the traditional thinking you relied upon earlier. That was fine for your needs list, but a wants list, which dominates in this stage, requires a little finesse. Often the money issues have been agreed upon already and it is the other issues that come into play.

Even in show business, which appears to be *all* about money, people find themselves in serious contention over problems that have nothing to do with money. In the 1950s, the most popular comedy on television was *I Love Lucy*, which is still seen in reruns today. Few people know that it would never have premiered at all had it not been for some very off-the-wall solutions to some very sticky problems.

First of all, this was 1951, and CBS television didn't want Desi Arnaz as part of the show. Why would they? Although he was one of the most successful bandleaders of his day, he was Cuban at a time when such mixed-ethnicity marriages were not widely accepted. Furthermore, he had no acting experience. CBS maintained that the public would have no interest in a comedy show about an interracial couple. Lucy had no reason to believe that she would make more money if her husband was in the show; she just wanted to spend more time with him. Lucy and Desi got the network to agree that if they could prove that their working together would be a hit with viewers, it would air the show. So the couple put together a traveling vaudeville act with themselves as the stars. The live audiences loved it, and CBS had to relent.

The next snag occurred when it came to naming the show. CBS wanted to capitalize on Lucy's popularity as a radio and movie star by calling the program *The Lucille Ball Show*. Lucy wanted to show Desi respect by making sure his name was in the title, too. Again, not about money. The network refused until Desi suggested the title *I Love Lucy*, which obviously referred to him, although not by name.

Everything seemed to be on track until CBS told Lucy that the network wanted to broadcast the show live from New York as it did with all its other programming. Lucy wanted to stay on the West Coast with Desi, and, again, the show nearly died until Desi suggested filming it in Hollywood in front of a live studio audience. This rather creative suggestion seemed to solve the problem, except that CBS refused to pay for the extra costs involved in filming, processing, editing, and shipping the finished films by plane from Hollywood to the network headquarters in New York each week. In a stroke of brilliance, Desi negotiated a deal whereby he and Lucy would cover all these costs but would retain the right to rebroadcast the shows at a future date. Money *was* involved this time, but it was secondary to location. Lucy wanted to spend more time with her family in California. CBS readily agreed, since reruns were virtually unknown at the time. After all, who'd want to see a TV show more than once? These rights seemed worthless, so the network was more than willing to give them up.

The rest, as they say, is history. The show went on to be a huge hit, and the rerun rights made Lucy and Desi wealthy—all because of a lot of creative negotiating. Not only did Lucy get her need met of starring in a TV show, she got her wants met as well: She got her nonactor husband to be her costar, she got to stay on the West Coast with Desi, and they both got the rerun rights.

We can clearly see from this story that money is not always the most important issue. In fact, black belt negotiators look for as many nonmonetary concessions as possible to make the agreement a good deal for them. Common nonmonetary issues include delivery date, warranty, packaging, alteration, location, and service. Keep these and other such negotiating points in mind as you try to find middle ground.

Most people focus on money because it's so easy to do. You must remember that money is only a tool. Sellers only want money for the things it can buy. In one way or another, they're trying to solve a problem. If you can find out the real reason someone wants money now, you can reach his or her vital striking point. For instance, if you discover that home sellers are about to lose their properties to foreclosure, they might be willing to sell at a loss, just to save their credit rating.

When the deal is just about money it's hard to be creative because, as we said, money only goes up or down. The reason it is defined as a *common* form of exchange is that everyone understands its value. If you want to leverage a better deal for yourself, you must find things that have great value for you but less for your opponent. You can't do that with money because $100 holds the same purchasing power for you as it does for the other person. However, a delivery time could be very valuable to you and meaningless to the retailer you're purchasing from. If you have the least doubt that time is a critical component for a lot of people, just consider what Federal Express can charge to deliver a package overnight as opposed to its competitors.

THREE STEPS FOR FINDING MIDDLE GROUND

After you have sparred with your opponent for a while, you gain a sense of the person's strengths and weaknesses. In this part of the contest you should concentrate on your strengths and minimize your weaknesses.

In bargaining, you have already set aside virtually all the issues you both agree upon. Now it's time to focus on the areas of disagreement and narrow them down to a manageable few. If you don't do this, the deal will seem unwieldy. Everyone's focus can now be put to good use by developing specific solutions.

First, even with issues that are associated with conflict, there are always areas of agreement. If nothing else, you could just agree about what you both *disagree* about. In this case, walking away is probably the wisest course of action.

Taking the time to come together on a few points sets a positive tone and lets you see clearly how many areas of disagreement you still have to deal with.

Second, work through disagreements one at a time, starting with the most difficult issue first so it doesn't become an impasse later. Now this becomes the question: Are any of these wants a deal breaker for you or the other party? If so, you may just decide to walk away. People can be so attached to their wants that they appear to be needs, and they won't let go no matter what. Remember, though, that if you are going to tell other parties you believe they don't really need something, you had better do it with diplomacy. After all, they *believe* they need it.

Third, single out one disagreement and ask for possible solutions. Each disagreement that is settled brings you one step closer to the final agreement. Try not to focus on the enormity of the task in front of you because sometimes the length of your list can be daunting and make you feel discouraged. Remember: A journey of a thousand miles begins with a single step. Whatever you do, don't let your attention drift away from getting your wants list taken care of; in the blink of an eye, you can miss an opportunity. The biggest danger at this stage is letting your mind wander to the end of the deal and not finishing this part completely.

TECHNIQUES FOR BUYERS AND SELLERS

Before you can wrap up and move to the final round, you must get your opponent to commit to some or all of your proposals. Here are a few techniques that will help you accomplish this.

You Are the Seller

Let's say you are in the business of raising and selling those cute Chinese shar-pei puppies with all the wrinkles. A prospective buyer has driven forty-five miles to your farm to see your latest litter of six puppies, which you normally sell for $1,500 each. However, your research shows that presently there is a glut of this breed on the market. You need to sell at least one just to pay the bills, and the buyer has already agreed to buy a male puppy for $1,400. Ideally, you would like to sell her two dogs and turn a real profit.

ASK A CLOSED-ENDED QUESTION: Earlier we saw the power of using open-ended questions to obtain *information*. Now it's time to use closed-ended questions, to which the person must give a specific answer, in order to obtain *commitment*. Try asking the buyer, "How many puppies were you thinking about buying?" She might say one, as she did in the original conversation. But she might hedge her bets and say she isn't sure. Now you know there is an opening.

GIVE ALTERNATIVES OF YOUR OWN CHOOSING: You might say to the purchaser, "Would you want a male or female pup to go with this one?" You don't care what the answer is as long as it isn't "Neither one," in which case you may have to go to the next technique.

SWEETEN THE DEAL: Try saying, "If you take the black one now for thirteen hundred dollars, we'll give you a free day of obedience training. We normally charge two hundred dollars for this class." You know that adding another dog to a class costs you nothing, but it is valuable to her. Also, she might sign up for the whole series of classes if she likes the first one.

SHOW THEM AN EMPTY WELL: Ancient Chinese farmers would prove to tax collectors that they had nothing left to give the emperor by showing that their wells were dry. You can do the same by telling the other party, "As you know, we normally sell these AKC registered puppies for fifteen hundred dollars. After paying for all the examinations, shots, and food, plus our staff time to house-train them, we're only left with one thousand dollars. Then don't forget the cost of our mortgage, utilities, and our own time. We really can't go any lower without losing money."

GIVE THE ILLUSION OF PRECISION: Quoting buyers round numbers as a sales price or offering sellers round numbers as a purchase price implies that that you still have more to give. In our example with the puppies, offering to drop your price from $1,500 to $1,300 suggests to the buyer that you might be willing to go to $1,250 or even $1,200. Instead, try telling her that $1,329 is your best price. The exactness of this number sounds as if you've calculated all of your costs and that truly is the best you can do. Even an experienced negotiator would have difficulty justifying asking you to drop another $29 now.

TURN MOUNTAINS INTO MOLEHILLS: There's another ancient Chinese proverb that says, "Those who remove mountains begin by carrying away small stones." In other words, break a large expense into small pieces to make it more palatable to the buyer. For instance you could say, "I know that thirteen hundred dollars seems like a lot of money, but if you charge it to your credit card and pay it off over a year's time, that would only come to less than four dollars a day. Heck, a fancy cup of coffee costs as much as that. Would you be willing to give up just one cup of coffee in exchange for a loyal and lovable companion for years to come?"

PUT THE OTHER PARTY IN YOUR SHOES: It has been said, "I felt sorry for myself because I had no shoes, until I met a man who had no feet." Help the other person understand your position by letting her experience it. "If you were in our business and were only going to make fifty dollars after expenses, would *you* be willing to lower *your* price?"

USE THE PUPPY DOG CLOSE: With certain products, getting them into the hands of the customer makes the most sense. It's hard to return a puppy once you have grown attached to it. Try saying to the buyer, "Look, I know you're not sure that you want two dogs. Take them both home for the weekend, and if you don't want the other one after that, just bring her back with no obligation." Who could return one of these lovable creatures after watching them play together? What happens to the argument over price once the buyer emotionally owns the other puppy?

You Are the Buyer

Let's say it's always been your dream as a couple to retire and drive around the country for a few years. This means you're in the market for a high-end recreational vehicle. You've settled on the model you can afford, but now you're faced with an avalanche of options that would make living in the RV just that much nicer. You put on your wants list the following:

- Dinette with four chairs
- Flat-screen TV in the bedroom
- Convection microwave

- Tinted windows
- Power seats for driver and passengers
- Exterior foldout awning
- Secondary air-conditioning unit for extra cooling
- Cherrywood kitchen cabinets

EMPTY POCKETS: The dealer quotes you a price of $10,000 for the package of extras. Flatly tell her that's way above your budget. She'll probably say the best she can do is $8,000. That's not a bad price reduction just for pleading poverty.

FALSE DEADLINE: You might suggest that you have somewhere to go soon and will come back later. Every car and RV salesperson is trained never to let customers leave because the chances of them ever coming back are small. She might offer to throw in an upgrade to cherry wood cabinets if you buy now.

FOCUS ON THE FUTURE: Let the dealer know that you have many friends who are also thinking about retiring and traveling. You would be willing to refer them, but you need a better deal on those options for which you know she has a large profit margin.

ASK THE QUESTION AGAIN: When she offers you an answer, try asking the same question again. This implies that the initial response was unacceptable. Questions such as "How much did you say the option package cost?" or "Could you explain that one more time?" or "Will you run that by me again?" can be incredibly powerful because they act like a flinch, especially if you ask them in an incredulous manner. It makes the salesperson rethink the legitimacy of her offer and prompts her to do better. Doing this also gives you time to reconsider your position, and you may change the deal in your mind while she is still answering you.

HAND THEM YOUR PROBLEM: You can simply say to the dealer, "All we have is six thousand dollars in our budget for the options." Then be silent. This puts the pressure on the dealer to find a solution.

AN INCH OF TIME: A Chinese proverb says, "An inch of time cannot be bought with an ounce of gold." Salespeople are acutely aware of their time because they are generally compensated on commission and not salary. The longer this salesperson spends with you trying to make a sale, the less money she earns in an hour. The pressure is on her to close the deal and move on to another customer. Just be patient and allow the time to do its work.

WHAT ARE THE CONSEQUENCES IF NEGOTIATIONS FAIL?

In martial arts, the more important the contest is to both fighters, the more likely it is that a challenge is going to be accepted to meet in the ring. The more emotionally invested they become, either because of their own mental commitment or as a result of the urging of others, the more likely the contest will actually take place. In other words, when others are watching there is more pressure to follow through, whereas when they're just bragging among themselves they can more easily walk away. And finally, the greater the consequences of a failure, the more likely it is that an agreement will occur because neither side can afford to lose the deal. Whenever there is little to gain, no one cares one way or the other, so it's harder to keep everyone at the table long enough to put a deal together.

As we can see, once you reach the midpoint of a negotiation, the consequences of failing have increased because of two important factors: time and emotions. The emotional component is important everywhere, but in non-negotiating cultures, where "time equals money," time often trumps emotions.

Since your needs have already been satisfied at this point, there is good reason for you to stay invested; you have begun to mentally *own* the transaction. If you are the seller in a transaction, you've begun to see yourself spending the money you will receive. If you're the buyer, you are picturing yourself enjoying the product or service you are bartering for. The cost of walking away has become very high.

However, experienced negotiators will tell you that when the stakes are this high and the parties are equally powerful, these deals are the most difficult to structure. It's hard for either side to gain leverage, so these deals often end in a stalemate—in spite of the fact that an agreement would present many benefits to each party.

When I was the chairman of the board of a credit union, we were always looking for other credit unions to merge with to increase our economies of scale and service to our members. Merging in smaller member-owned financial institutions is relatively easy because they can see the benefits that a larger credit union has to offer—a greater choice of products and services and more branches. The most difficult mergers to accomplish were between equal-sized credit unions because both had less motivation to join together and both had equal power with which to assert their needs. As a result of this power dynamic, our credit union merged with over a dozen smaller companies during a twenty-year period but repeatedly failed to partner with equivalent-sized institutions.

One issue that I do not encounter very often in high-level bargaining is inexperienced negotiators. However, it's very common in everyday bargaining situations. One scenario you may run into is other parties still bargaining for their needs, even at this stage, because most amateur hagglers don't have a logical negotiating plan. They have no idea they're supposed to get their needs out of the way in the first stage. This puts the professional negotiator in the driver's seat because people will give up many of their wants to get a critical need met. The beauty of being in this position for you is that you are now dealing only with your wants. Everything you win is just icing on the cake. If the other parties are still dealing with their needs, you are in a very strong bargaining position.

12

Distance Yourself from the Battle

The angry man will defeat himself in battle as in life.
SAMURAI SAYING

Frustration occurs when we have been thwarted. Either we want something to happen and it doesn't or we don't want something to happen and it does. Anger is an emotional state induced by displeasure.

Martial artists are engaged in a fight that involves a very narrow range of communication and one goal: to win. There are two prevailing emotions that can occur. The first is frustration because it is so easy to be thwarted; your kick can be blocked, a punch can be missed, or your opponent's kicks and punches can hit their mark consistently. Frustration leads to the second emotion—anger. Whenever you are thwarted many times in a row, frustration builds. If there is no release (in a match, this would mean by scoring points), it soon turns into outright anger.

Either one of these emotions can act like a stick of dynamite to your peace of mind and composure during a contest, causing you to forget your training. This can be deadly to a fighter. Everything in a match is happening so fast; you have to rely on your training to win because there is no time to stop and think about what's happening and what to do next. Your focus cannot be distracted by high emotions. Once your emotions are out of the way, your training will flow automatically.

When we think of flow, the first thing that comes to mind is water. Water can be many things: gentle yet powerful, still yet in motion, floating and floated upon, heavy yet light, invisible and visible, solid or vapor. "Water people," as they are called in the Far East, are a perfect illustration of this paradox. They are soft on the outside and strong on the inside. There is an old saying in the West: "Let it flow off your back," which means "don't let it bother you." Whatever comes up in your life, and whatever emotions an event triggers, let it flow right off of you. This is the meaning of detachment.

When you are negotiating, you must be emotionally detached. If you take offhanded remarks or an aggressive offer too personally, you will lose. This is why professional negotiators live by the saying "Lose your composure, lose the negotiation." When your composure goes, you will become distracted from your objectives and goals and you will become unbalanced.

It is easy to see why a buyer or seller might become a little too attached to the outcome of a negotiation. But you might wonder why real estate agents and attorneys, who act on behalf of a client, often become so emotionally involved in the outcome of a negotiation. After all, they are only intermediaries who transmit information between the various parties. Agents are not buying or selling the home themselves, and attorneys aren't going to receive any award directly from a jury. The most obvious reason, then, is that they're thinking about their commission or contingency fee.

In a bargaining situation, this is the worst possible thing you can do. If you want to win too badly, it means you have too much to lose. Desperation makes for very poor motivation because it causes you to lose your perspective—and your cool.

WOMEN AND EMOTIONS

Interestingly, Sensei Tabuchi says that he's noticed that women fighters tend to spar with much more detachment and much less emotion than men. The reason, he believes, is that they have less ego and testosterone involved in a match. However, during a negotiation, women must watch their emotions as much as any man because they tend to take what the other party says and does too personally.

Emotions can be a valuable weapon, but they must be used at just the right time, and you must still be in control at all times. The wrong time for a woman to become volatile is when the talks are going her way, because an outburst will stop the forward motion. She should be careful not to go overboard on some topic that is relatively unimportant to her just because she is offended by something her opponent says. It will throw a wrench in the works at precisely the wrong time.

There are times, though, when she (or a man, for that matter—which can be even more unsettling because no one sees it coming) can use the tendency to become impassioned to her own advantage. A woman who is reacting emotionally during a bargaining session will make any man in the room very uncomfortable. On the one hand, this can be disastrous if it causes both parties to lose sight of their goals. On the other hand, it could be a deliberate tool to shift the momentum in the direction of her goals. When a woman is having a mini-meltdown, a man will give a lot to end the display. This is not a tactic that will appeal to every woman because it fits too easily into stereotypes, but for those who are so inclined, now is the time to ask for the moon and the stars because you might at least get the stars. A woman can also use her emotions as a distraction if her opponent is coming too close to one of her striking points.

It must be pointed out, though, that you can effectively use an emotional outburst only once. After that, it loses its effectiveness and may even seem contrived.

If you are a man who doesn't want to accidentally trigger an emotional outburst when bargaining with a woman, you should avoid a few things. According to *Women and the Art of Negotiating*, by Juliet Nierenberg, certain very specific behaviors almost always make women angry:

- Condescension
- Bullying
- Being treated as superfluous
- Having their views ignored
- Being overprotected
- Being given the "pet" treatment ("Aren't you adorable?")
- Being passed over in a conversation in favor of another

It is wise for men to keep these words in mind because many top female negotiators, just like masters in martial arts, do not get mad. They get even. Don't provoke a fight you cannot win just because your mind is stuck back in the 1950s.

Similarly, women should avoid certain behaviors that almost always make men angry, unless you deliberately want to rile them up:

- Wounding their ego
- Hurting their pride
- Questioning their masculinity
- Treating them like children

ANGER

In the martial arts, emotions can be used as a tactic. Your opponent may deliberately slap you in the face just to make you mad. The same can hold true at the bargaining table. Some negotiators will play into your emotions to make you lose your composure on purpose. It's unfair but true. They might say something derogatory about you, your client, your product, or your offer, just to rile you up. To avoid falling for this amateurish trick, you will need to understand why it works and what you can do about it.

Asians believe that control over the body *is* control over the mind. There are several physical moves you can make to shake off an emotional state: (1) Laugh. Breaking out in laughter breaks the tension—yours and theirs. (2) Take a deep breath. This gives you time to collect yourself and relax. (3) Quickly tense all the muscles in your body and then let go. This also releases tension and allows your mind to detach from emotional entanglement.

Previously I said that it could be a mistake to provoke martial arts masters because they won't get mad, they'll get even. Only the top people, those who have mastered their craft, can control their emotions to this degree. Most of us mere mortals are subject to them and can be manipulated by them. That's why Sensei Tabuchi often tells his students to push the envelope and press a frustrated person toward the brink—you can use the fact that the person's emotions are out of control. He knows that most people lose sight of their objectives when they're in the heat of rage, and that is precisely the moment for you to move in and score points. People who are in the grip of anger feel as if they are somehow stronger, but that's just the adrenaline talking. In reality, enraged people are helpless people. They might feel they are having a burst of physical strength, but it is actually a moment of mental weakness, one that their opponents can exploit if they know how. You must also turn this wisdom around and keep yourself from hitting an emotional hotpoint. Instead, flow like water around any obstacle.

The most effective countertactic you can utilize is to concentrate on your important issues. Go back to your lists of wants and needs to ground yourself in reality and make sure you are focusing on the right objectives.

While angry people are ranting, they are probably handing their opponents a great deal of information they don't mean to. They are, in fact, exposing their vital striking points. In addition to this liability, they have rendered themselves unable to notice anything new about their opponents. Studies show that when the brain is pumped up with anger, it shuts down the ability to take in information. Watch two people who are screaming at each other. Neither one can hear a thing the other person is saying. Try telling something to a six-year-old who is having a tantrum. It doesn't work. The child can't understand you until he or she calms down.

Bruce Lee understood the power of emotions. He would be in a fight and his opponent would hit him. Instead of snarling back, Lee would simply respond with a smile. It was as if he was saying, "You can't hurt me." This would infuriate his opponents, and soon they would grow frustrated and flail wildly at him just to land a kick or a punch. Their fury only made it easier for him to block their unfocused blows and take them out with one of his own.

Black belts learn to channel their own frustration away from anger and into increased focus. At the same time, they look for any small opening in their opponent and exploit it over and over again. It's like a tiny drop of water falling onto a solid rock. At first, it seems to have no effect, but if the droplets continue over time, they can eventually split any boulder.

One of the biggest fears that new negotiators harbor is that a situation will explode out of control. They're afraid that the other party will become angry for one reason or another, and they will have to figure out a way to deal with it. Far from being a disadvantage to you, this situation can be filled with opportunity if you know how to handle it.

Bruce Lee had his own reasons for encouraging anger in his opponents. He used it to upset their composure. Ironically, prompting the anger to come out can have the opposite effect, too. Giving people permission to blow off steam leads to a situation in which they begin to empty themselves of anger. After a time, doing this will diffuse the anger completely.

When people are angry, they only want to be heard. The worst thing you can do at this moment is try to "fix" the problem. And yet this is the approach most men take all the time. You barely get three words out of your mouth about why you're mad, and the man is throwing out answers and solutions that you haven't asked for. If you go on expressing your discontent, he often becomes more insistent that you stop and listen to him tell you what to do about it. Women understand instinctively that this is not an approach that works, because people who are letting off steam aren't asking for help or advice; they are asking to be listened to. So give them what they want. Simply listen, make a few notes, and then be silent.

When people first erupt, the natural reaction is to respond in kind by yelling back, which only serves to escalate the confrontation. Instead of giving in to the urge, let them finish their initial statement and take a few notes on why they are angry. When they come up for air, say, "I can see that you're unhappy. Is there anything else you're upset about?" Just as you did before, take notes. They will wind up again, but this time, they'll start in at a lower level of anger because so much steam has already been released. Letting go of anger doesn't happen all at once. It may take a few bouts before they are finished. Every time they want to continue talking about their grievances, just repeat these steps: Listen, take notes, and ask for more issues by saying, "I understand. What else made you mad?" Don't start talking yourself until they feel they have been completely heard. You don't want to cut them off because the only thing angry people want is to keep talking until they are finished.

Once they are genuinely finished and have dissipated all their anger, they have created somewhat of a vacuum. This is an auspicious moment for you because in the face of your equanimity, they realize how badly they have behaved. They may be apologetic and embarrassed, a very pliable state. Apologetic people will give you a lot to make up for their excessive display of emotion.

At this point, calmly go over your notes and address the issues that upset them. This does not mean that you have to agree to anything on the list, but you must talk about the issues to show that you were listening. The bonus in making the list is that not only does it make your opponents feel that you were taking them seriously enough to write everything down, but it gives you the opportunity to take note of their vital striking points, which they have been busy handing you on a silver platter.

BLUE BELT TEST

In Chapters 10–12 you learned how to respond to an initial offer, establish common ground, and stay emotionally uninvolved in the bargaining process. Now it's time to put all this knowledge to work in a very safe and fun way. You will not spend more than $20, you will end up with something that you can use, and you will get a chance to practice your negotiating skills.

Go to a garage sale in your area and bargain on several small items that you might find useful around your home or office. Spend no more than $20. Afterward, answer the following questions:

1. Did you get the other party to make the first offer?
2. Were you aware of resistance when you made an offer or counteroffer?
3. Did you show interest in something other than your primary target first?
4. Did you flinch at proposals?
5. Did you reject the first offer?
6. Did you get all your needs met before moving to your wants?
7. Did you consider issues other than money during the negotiations?
8. Did you use the "illusion of precision" or another technique?
9. Did you consider the consequences if negotiations failed?
10. Did you keep your emotions under control?
11. What emotions came up for you during the bargaining?
12. What emotions did you notice in the other party during negotiations?
13. Did you make assumptions that you wish you hadn't?
14. Did you walk away? How did it feel?

Evaluate how you ranked with this negotiation exercise. If there were aspects that you want to improve, strive to work on those at the next opportunity. There's always another garage sale somewhere.

There were a lot of powerful techniques in this section that must be practiced to master. Write down just one skill that you want to improve and make that the focus of your next negotiation.

PART V

Red Belt

The sun is setting. The first phase of growth has been accomplished.

This is the most dangerous stage for a martial arts student. A person who has achieved a Red Belt knows that he and his fellow students can generate immense power but have not yet mastered control over it. It's little comfort when Sensei Tabuchi admits publicly that he has had his nose broken more often by red belts than any other group. In a negotiation, the stakes are also high, a lot of work has already gone into the process, and there is much to lose if one fails. The Red Belt negotiator resorts to his very best moves, and he becomes mentally engaged at the top level of his ability.

One aspect that a Red Belt becomes supremely aware of is time. He learns to keep track how far into a round he's at and what he must do to win that round with the time remaining. In Chapter 13—"Making Time Your Ally"— readers will learn about the effect that deadlines have on the mind and pick up tips for using them to their advantage. Beginners often fall for false deadlines and lose points to their opponent. The experienced Red Belt does not make this mistake.

At this stage of his studies, the martial artist becomes much more sophisticated. He grows into advanced concepts about how to focus his own attention and use it like a weapon. He also dips into an egoless state, which gives him great power because it lets him toss aside the baggage of his persona and fight totally in the here-and-now. In Chapter 15—"Developing Advanced Fighting Skills"—Red Belt negotiators will learn the secrets of the East and find out how these subtle ideas and tactics will help him win, even over a superior opponent.

Negotiators and fighters alike find, as the match draws closer to its end, that definite barriers arise and must be dealt with. In Chapter 15—"Breaking Impasses"—I identify these barriers and show how an experienced fighter shatters them. Neophytes fall into deep disappointment when they reach an impasse caused by seemingly impenetrable obstacles, but the seasoned veteran knows how to reach into his bag of tricks and try something new. Many bargaining sessions reach an impasse. If at least one party does not know how to break through it, the negotiation is over. Both sides lose.

13

Making Time
Your Ally

Time can be your best friend or your worst enemy.
MICHAEL SOON LEE

In martial arts tournaments there are usually three rounds of three minutes each, but you shouldn't wait until the last minute of the final round to use your best techniques. First of all, you'll be tired out by then and won't execute them skillfully. Second, it will be obvious to your opponents that you've saved your best stuff for last, and they will be ready for it. If they're ahead on points, they know they can just evade you and there is little you can do to win. If they're behind, they'll know to wait for you to expend the last of your energy and then leverage their own blows for maximum effect once your guard is down. Time changes the way people think in any contest. They make different decisions depending upon their perception of how much is available to them.

People think about time in distinct ways in different areas of the world, and there is no more stark contrast than between the East and the West. Americans, Swiss, and Germans are among the most time-conscious people in the world, and they often confirm this by saying things like "Time is money." Conversely, Asians have a much more relaxed attitude about it and use this old saying: "With time and patience the mulberry leaf becomes a silk gown." In other words, you're not necessarily going to get what you want right this minute. But if you are willing to wait, you will.

In the West we think of time as *monochronic,* meaning that it marches forward in a very linear way from birth to death. In contrast, people in the East consider time to be *polychronic,* whereby it is cyclical; it begins every day, ends at night, and restarts the next day. Monochronic people tend to do one task at a time and take schedules and deadlines very seriously, whereas polychronic people can do many things at once. They might have schedules and deadlines, but they aren't wedded to them.

The best place to see time conflicts in action is during international negotiations. When I and another American were negotiating television broadcast rights in Japan, we were always early for appointments, while our Japanese counterparts were habitually late. We wanted to talk about one issue at a time, while they tried to group several together. We felt a need to finish the discussions and then relax, while our hosts talked a little, partied a little, talked some more, and partied some more. It nearly drove us crazy until we realized that this was just a different way of viewing time.

Westerners tend to equate time with money, whereas in the East, they espouse the philosophy that time is for building relationships. If you want to be a strong negotiator, you don't need to be from the East, but you can borrow some of their ideas about time because they are certainly right about one thing: Successful deals are built on good relationships.

RULES OF DEADLINES

A deadline is a date or time before which something must be done. I have coined a new term, *dealine*™, which is a date or time before which a negotiation *must be* completed. Time can work either for or against you in these situations.

In negotiations there are six rules of dealines that can help you end up with a better deal.

1. A Real Dealine Is the Soonest a Negotiation Will Conclude

Most negotiations do not have a set dealine. When you walk into an appliance store to buy a washer and dryer, you generally have no idea when you are going to leave. It is an informal, spontaneous bargaining session.

In other situations, though, it is understood that a dealine must be set, and the minute you do, the whole energy around the bargaining process changes. Now time is a factor. When this happens, good negotiators become more focused, while the poor ones grow sloppy because of the pressure. Since you know this, you can be ready to take advantage of any opportunities that may arise as a result of the other person's diminished capacity.

You'll notice I said that the soonest a negotiation will finish is when you approach a "real" dealine. Not all dealines are genuine. For example, when you walk into a store, the dealine to buy is theoretically whenever it closes. However, wouldn't the store stay open to make a big sale? If the salesperson is on commission, it most certainly would; however, if the person is just an order taker, then probably not. Here's where spying on your opponent would be valuable. Before you start seriously bargaining, find out how the salespeople earn their pay. You can use the pressure of the store closing and the fear of a lost sale only if it means a loss of commission.

The closing time is obviously a dealine the store imposes on its customers. Is there anything you could do to establish your own? You could let the salesperson know that you planned to visit a competitor in an hour; this puts pressure on him or her to make a deal before you leave. This may or may not be true, but it will still serve its purpose. If you can set up soft (movable) dealines and pass them off as hard (immovable), you can achieve the same results as if there was a real one.

Dealines are a challenge not only in a negotiation. Most of us deal with them in the workplace all the time. One of the biggest challenges is when you have coworkers or even bosses who just don't meet dealines. They never have, and they're not going to start now. I used to tell my boss that if I didn't hear back by a time we both agreed to, then I would take that as a green light to go ahead with whatever we had been discussing. Eventually she realized that I took dealines seriously, and she began to let me know whether she had a problem with something before the drop-dead date.

2. Test the Dealine to See If It's Real

When people set a dealine for you, they could be trying to fake you out. Most dealines turn out to be soft and can be moved, so test them to see how real (hard) they are. You can do this by asking why, exactly, the other party needs a decision by that hour? Where did the deadline come from and what happens if you don't meet it? Or you can call the person's bluff by letting the dealine pass, and then see what happens. Usually, it's absolutely nothing. In Chapter 9 you learned to tell what the truth looks like. Use the same skill when testing for real versus soft dealines.

Remember, a real dealine cannot be moved because there is an actual reason for it. If you need tables, chairs, and silverware for your wedding, you need the vendor to have it there on time. Obviously, you're not going to move your wedding date because the caterer can't find your chairs. The further in advance that everybody is aware of the dealine, the better it is. Then there's more time to prepare, and everyone knows just how much time there is to hedge, waver, and fool around before they have to get serious.

3. The One Who Has the Least Time Pressure Usually Wins

In martial arts contests, fighters who are behind must fight not only their opponents but the clock as well. You must push yourself to win points to even the score but also to win an extra one to be victorious.

When negotiating, if there is a dealine you really have to meet, then it works against you. As the dealine approaches, if you are in a position where you have won all of your needs and a good number of your wants, then there is little pressure on you. However, if you've still got unfinished business as the buzzer is about to sound and you're not at all satisfied with the deal, all the pressure will be on you to do something—anything—to win a few points. The side with the least pressure can bide its time to wait for the other to cave in.

Generally, if you're the one to set the dealine, you have the power to control it by either sticking to it or extending it. If the other party sets it, you are at their mercy and may have to give concessions to get them to change it. Obviously though, this is not black-and-white.

Treat negotiating like a Scholastic Aptitude Test (SAT) in which you know you have only a limited amount of time. Students have to plan to answer more than half the questions by the halfway mark so they have time to review their work. This is why at this stage of the negotiations you must make sure your biggest wants are met so that time doesn't become a factor, because most concessions are given just before the dealine.

4. Put Your Opponent Under Time Pressure

When bargaining, it's vital that you create time pressures for the other party; otherwise, the bargaining will drag on and on. It's a well-known fact in the legal profession that most lawsuits are settled on the courthouse steps just before a trial is about to begin. Why? Because the minute the disagreeing parties enter the courtroom, their costs go up dramatically. Suddenly, they are faced with the expenses of judges, juries, court reporters, bailiffs, expert witnesses, depositions, discovery, and more. The trial date is the dealine no one really wants to face.

Try to develop a dealine for the other party even if the person doesn't already have one. For instance, if you are selling a used car, let the buyer know that other interested parties are coming to look at it later that evening. If you are the one who is buying, schedule several appointments in a row so you can honestly tell the seller that you are looking at other cars shortly. Most people say something nonspecific like "I need to have an answer by tomorrow night at five," which is a soft dealine. In this case, no specific reasons were given. However, dealines are more believable and compelling when you provide a logical reason for making them. If you don't offer them, the other parties will probably realize this was just a strategy to force their hand and they'll see right through it.

As human beings, we have a tendency to wait until the last minute to do anything that is not urgent. Why do you think there is always such a long line at the post office on April 15, with people trying to get their tax returns postmarked by the due date? It's not as if they didn't know it was coming. Since you know that people put themselves under pressure like this, be sure you're not doing the same. Then you can use their panic against them and get them to agree to points they otherwise wouldn't have.

Also, be aware that when there is a dealine, most people become very reactive. Don't be one of them. Master negotiators are able to practice *mushin* because they are not being manipulated by time and can be open to all possibilities and focused all at the same time.

5. The Longer Negotiations Go On, the Less Likely There Will Be a Clear Resolution

The power of a hard dealine is that it ends all further negotiations. When it's over, it's over. If you allow bargaining to drag on, goals can become muddy, more wants are thrown into the mix, and people become emotionally attached to unreasonable positions.

A protracted war is an example of what can happen when negotiations are not concluded promptly. The peace talks about the Vietnam War began in May 1968 without any specific dealine. The negotiations were subject to many lengthy delays, and, as a result, hostilities did not end until seven years later, in April 1975. During this time, senseless issues, such as the shape of the negotiating table, became stumbling blocks, while thousands of people died during the fighting.

6. Don't Just Accept Last-Minute Dealines

In Chapter 5, we learned to ask well ahead of time whether there are any dealines we should be aware of. However, some sly opponents, as a negotiating tactic, will not tell you they're there until the very last moment. This places you in the position of having to scramble and think quickly on your feet, which not everyone can do. If you feel that this new information puts you under too much pressure, you may just be better off walking away. Only if you're already very satisfied with the deal you've put together so far is it really worth staying.

If you do find yourself surprised by a dealine that appears out of nowhere, the first step is to flinch. Act shocked, surprised, and disappointed. This tells the other party how unacceptable and unethical you find his or her behavior. Remember to be quiet after you have flinched, to let the other party react. It gives people the chance to take back or modify their time limit.

In a martial arts tournament and in negotiations, the one who uses time most effectively usually wins. In bargaining, you must be focused yet relaxed as the dealine approaches. As mentioned in Chapter 12, "Distancing Yourself from the Battle," it's important not to become emotionally involved in the negotiations or you could lose track of time and your objectives.

14

Developing Advanced Fighting Skills

Minor details can determine the outcome of a major battle.
SUN-TZU

Once martial artists have proved, over the course of many years, that they will be diligent about their studies, that they'll stick to their practice, that they are loyal and trustworthy, they finally have earned the right to enter the realm of advanced fighting. Here they will be shown the most powerful, almost mystical techniques that can give them an edge in any situation. It's a world of seeming contradictions and endless possibilities.

Some of martial arts' secret skills are only to be used in life-and-death situations. There are extraordinary techniques such as one-punch knockouts that can render an opponent unconscious with one blow and nerve strikes that can make an attacker's arm or leg useless by shutting down the nerves and interrupting the flow of *ki* (energy). These require extreme precision and years of practice to perfect.

Yet the ultimate secret weapon is only whispered about in back alleys. That is the *death blow.* It can stop an assailant's heart with a single punch. I have witnessed this amazing feat as a scientific demonstration with a team of doctors present to revive the subjects. It is a frightening yet awesome sight. You can see why only the most elite fighters are entrusted with this kind of knowledge. At this stage, martial arts masters take ordinary human abilities to an extraordinary level.

Some secret tactics can be legally and ethically used in tournaments, but others cannot. At this level, traditional techniques are refined to a high art and give fighters a tremendous advantage over their competition. However, to accomplish them, you must know the art so well that you don't have to think about it. To reach this level, you must be able to put the ego aside and let your training take over.

Now that you have arrived at this chapter, you have proved that you are no quitter in your quest to become a black belt negotiator. You have studied all the fundamentals of bargaining and practiced your skills, so you should be ready to learn advanced negotiating techniques. Although there are no *death blows* in bargaining, there are tactics that only the most experienced and dedicated professionals use, and I will reveal many of their secrets here. We begin with concepts and then move to actual tactics.

ADVANCED CONCEPTS

Laser Focus

Martial arts masters share their knowledge without selfish aims or intentions. Yes, a few want to brag about how many students or dojos they have, but most do it out of a genuine love of the art. Sensei Tabuchi, for example, wants to help people learn to defend themselves and become more physically fit and mentally strong. As a result, there is no hesitation in his actions because he is driven by a true sense of purpose.

A fight automatically triggers the ego. The body is being attacked, so the mind thinks, "I have to defend myself." This is a natural reaction, but it can sabotage a martial artist's game. The ego doesn't listen, is stubborn, and aims for short-term goals—all traits that work against a seamless performance in a tournament.

The ordinary mind is sometimes our worst enemy when we are trying to win a match. The reason we cannot transcend our ordinary mind is that it is the home of the seven deadly sins—pride, greed, lust, envy, gluttony, anger, and laziness. They anchor us in worldly desires, and the incessant mental noise they create keeps us from reaching inner stillness. These traits form the typical content of ego, which is fine for mundane tasks like washing the dishes. But martial artists who are competing at the highest level require a degree of concentration that the rest of life does not, and they need a mind that is capable of laser focus. We usually think of the seven deadly sins as a moral issue, but here they relate to performance. In their own way, every one of them interferes with excelling. The usual mind clutter, to which we are mostly oblivious, is actually far more distracting than we think. We can tell how much it really interferes only when we are required to operate at peak performance.

This isn't true just for martial artists. All kinds of sports—tennis, golf, baseball, basketball—now offer classes on the importance of and tactics for egoless focusing without the distractions of ordinary mind. The reason, simply, is that the usual mind clutter has to die down in order to take your game to the highest level.

When the ego is put aside, what emerges are the seven holy virtues: humility, chastity, abstinence, generosity, patience, kindness, and diligence. These are states of mind that cultivate a form of open awareness that allows for pinpoint focus in any contest.

When you get the ego out of the way, one physical faculty that improves enormously—that grows sharper—is hearing. Great martial artists can hear that their opponent is about to make a move before the person can unleash it. You can learn to recognize the sound coming from the elbow just as the punch is cocked or from the knee as the leg is pulled back for a kick. Masters often know all they need to know just by listening. In fact, sometimes at night Sensei Tabuchi will turn off all the lights in the dojo and let students spar in total darkness. This helps improve their hearing so not only can they detect where an opponent is, but they can plan what to do next.

Such advanced listening skills can be applied to negotiating as well. If you put your ego aside, you will start hearing things you never thought possible, such as what your opponent is *not* saying and what the person *doesn't* want you to know. The other party may not be telling you about his or her true needs and may not want you to know that he or she desperately needs you to accept the offer. You are no longer listening with your head but with your heart and intuition.

For many people, their egos are at the forefront of their awareness. This affects their perception of their needs and wants sometimes to such an extent that everything seems like a need and nothing is a want anymore. Everything begins to be a "must have," not a "maybe have." It's very hard to satisfy this kind of person. Egos are demanding, always tense, quick to anger, insatiable, full of themselves, and hard to teach because they think they know it all. This reminds me of the Zen master showing his student why he couldn't teach him. He took a glass that was already full to the brim with water, and then tried to pour more water in. Of course, the water he poured in just spilled over the side and onto the table. The point was clear: "You cannot fill a mind that is already full."

Egoless Meditation Exercise

The following is an exercise to put you into an egoless state. At first it will be very frustrating because thoughts will continually try to intrude. However, if you persevere in the practice, you'll find you can achieve this state at any time and in any place.

Find a quiet, dark place where you can sit for about half an hour with eyes closed. Place your hands in your lap with palms facing up as if ready to receive whatever comes your way. Try not to shift your body once you are seated because this engages the mind and puts you into the usual me-me-me state of mind.

Focus your attention on your breath as you slowly breathe in and out through your nose. With each breath, relax every part of your body, starting with your toes and working your way up to your head. Soon you will notice that thoughts will intrude into the clear space you have created, so just bring your focus back to your breath. If your attention wanders, do not give in to frustration because this is just your ego telling you that you "should" do better. Judgment is the antithesis of the egoless state, so just return your focus to your breathing. Wise practitioners tell beginners to think of how they would treat a baby. If a baby kept losing its attention and doing the same thing over and over, you wouldn't shake her or yell at her, even if you were frustrated. Instead, the infant would bring out endless kindness and patience in you. Gently, you would keep bringing her hand back, saying, "No, no" without harshness or blame. Why not treat yourself the same way? Instead of being impatient at your mind for losing concentration, gently keep bringing it back into focus. Eventually, you will train it.

Although this exercise might seem simple on paper, most people find it challenging in a way that no other task in their life has ever been. With everything else in life, you are trying to *do* something. Here, you are just trying to *be*. A famous philosopher once said that we may as well call ourselves "human doings" because we're doing something all the time. We don't know how to just be. Meditating, above all, is simply not doing. It's not a question of sitting on a meditation cushion and *doing* something different. It's *not* doing everything you usually do. Just stop doing, and see what happens.

You'll know when you've reach the egoless state because your senses begin to heighten. Of course, the minute you notice this, it will be gone, because noticing requires engaging the mind and the ego. Try to extend the egoless state for longer periods of time every time you sit, and try not to get mad at yourself, since, again, this requires ego.

Once you are able to maintain the egoless state, consistently begin to practice it in public—at lunch with friends, at a meeting with coworkers, on the bus, and in negotiating sessions. You'll be amazed at the sights, sounds, and thoughts you'll notice with your heightened sensitivity.

Letting Go of the Past

The ego is the container for your identity, which is the entity that holds on to your past. Holding on to your past is like carrying around a heavy burden and never setting it down. Wherever we go, whatever we do, we bear the weight of past events and what we believe they tell us about ourselves.

When we are in an egoless state, however, we are in the here and now and we are liberated from this burden. All the lenses that distort reality drop away, and we can see clearly what is in front of us. This means that martial artists can see their opponents without fear or the usual entrapments of identity. For negotiators, it means they can see their opponents clearly, too. If their past history usually saddles them with feelings of inferiority or low self-esteem, these will lift, and the negotiators will approach their counterparts with confidence. And clear vision allows negotiators' actions to be appropriate to the situation. In fact, all those who are grounded in the present moment experience more confidence because they are secure in themselves. This is the experience of pure willpower. "I know who I am and I know what I can do."

When the mind is unencumbered by the past, we can see just how brilliant we truly are. We get out of our own way and are able to see our options more clearly. In other words, the mind is razor sharp. Anything that will muddy our vision falls away, and what needs to be done stands out in sharp clarity.

I am sure it seems to some people that they need their ego, even with all its baggage, because it is the warrior side of themselves that will fight for their self-interest. The whole idea of being without an ego makes them feel defenseless. "Why," they ask, "would I want to be in an egoless state while negotiating?" If you think with an Eastern mind, though, you realize that you cannot be defeated when you have nothing to lose.

Our egos make us afraid to lose because we'll look silly or amateurish. Egoless people don't care about how they look, except for strategic purposes. Our egos don't want our opponents to win, whereas egoless people want others to win in their own way because they know that only by giving others what they want can they get what they need also. In other words, in an effort to emerge victorious from bargaining sessions, don't try to squash your opponents like a bug. You have to keep recognizing their humanity and treat them accordingly.

It takes a great deal of work to get into an egoless state, and even more practice to stay there. You must have the presence of mind to deliberately drop down into an almost meditative state. Although you still appear to function normally, your mind is allowed to float freely. One distinct aspect of this experience is that you are truly in the now. It's not as if your memory disappears, but the personal history you usually carry around as baggage drifts away and leaves you solely in the present moment.

People who learn to achieve this state of pure presence all arrive in a different way. This is not to say that they don't have an ego, because we all do, but being able to put it aside during a negotiation and at other times can be extremely powerful. Certainly we all have egos, and I am absolutely no exception.

I had a much bigger ego until I went through personal growth training back in the year 2000. I had hit rock bottom because, in spite of having a stellar career and what I thought was the perfect relationship, I was incredibly unhappy and desperately lonely. These feelings ate into my gut until I didn't care if I lived or died. Suddenly, I met a group of people who had very positive and open energy and whose presence just made me feel good. I eventually discovered that they had all been through a program that helped them to put their egos aside, and I decided I had nothing to lose if I did the same.

Frankly, it was torture. The facilitator was extremely intuitive and just seemed able to spot how each person's ego was getting in his or her way. For some, it was drugs, sex, or alcohol; for me, it was the need to project the image of a successful professional who was better than everyone else. I was forced to confront this and ask myself if I wanted others to see an empty facade or the true me—a scared little boy crying out for love.

We were also forced to look at who really ran our lives. I was absolutely sure that I was in control of my life until I examined my behaviors. I was a workaholic because I wanted approval from my father. I had a constant string of women in my life because I wanted love from my mother. I was afraid of commitment because I didn't want to relinquish control to another person since being abandoned by my first girlfriend when I was sixteen years old.

Instead of being the cool, controlling professional, I was actually being controlled by a lot of powerful figures from my past. Only by looking at each one of these people and making peace with them was I able to move on with my own life, not someone else's. Although I still work on this every day, I can honestly say that today I am more in control of my life than ever because I have found a way to let go of the past.

This is not a commercial for personal growth training. Everyone who becomes self-aware does it in a slightly different way because we have all had unique experiences and are distinct human beings. Some people let go of past history through meditation or therapy. Others come to it through religious experience, and still others read books and listen to CDs on the subject. There is no one correct path for everyone, including all the people who went through the same personal growth training as I did.

The interesting fact is that when you are able to get into this clear, calm state of being in the here and now, you can easily slip into the mind-set of your opponent. You are trying to hear what the other person is thinking not so you can take advantage of him or her but so you can hear the person's fears and problems. By doing so, you can soothe the person's angst and provide appropriate solutions. This leads to a deal that works for the other party and works for you.

Yes, you want to win. But that doesn't mean that you treat the other person like some *object* that you have to sweep out of the way so you can clean up and get everything you want. In the egoless state, you don't stop looking out for your own interests, but you nevertheless realize that the other person has interests, too. You recognize that just dismissing them out of hand would be toxic to the relationship.

Intuition

The top martial arts fighters just seem to have an extra edge, which is called *seeing with your skin*. It allows them to be open and sense the move their opponent is about to make before the opponent ever does it. You can imagine how invaluable a tool like this can be in a tournament. And yet this tool is available to everyone.

Have you ever had the feeling that the phone was about to ring, and it *did*? Not only that, but you felt you knew who was calling, and it *was* that person? These occurrences happen all the time, yet we often ignore them. They're called *moments of intuition*. The dictionary defines *intuition* as "the power or faculty of attaining direct knowledge or cognition without evident rational thought and inference." In other words, it is knowing something but not knowing *how* you know it. Some people trust their intuition and will act on it, while others dismiss it as a hunch and therefore not rational or believable information.

Asians seem to have developed more respect for this capacity than westerners. Many Asian religions refer to it as a great storehouse of knowledge in the universe that people can tap into if they are open to it. In the Western world we certainly acknowledge it, referring to it as a "gut feeling" or a "wild guess." It just doesn't have great status.

Almost all martial arts traditions espouse the development and use of intuition as a way to gain an edge over the competition. It is believed that the body knows what to do intuitively, and the best way to win is simply to *not* get in its way. You just know what the opponent's next move is going to be ahead of time and then react instantly.

If you are intuitive, you are able to see what the Japanese call *suki*, which literally means an opening, a gap. This is an unguarded moment in time that offers you the perfect opportunity to score points. But you don't have time to stop and think about it. You have to trust your intuitive judgment and act. If you know your craft well enough, you can trust it to work.

Negotiation, like the martial arts, is part art and part science. Sometimes you have research and information to rely upon, and other times you have only a gut feeling. More often than not, intuition will lead you down the right path when all the logic in the world tells you otherwise. At certain junctures, in fact, this is all you have to go on. The other party tells you something, and there's no time to go out and research whether it's the truth. And even if you could leave the table, you might not be able to find the information. You have to make a decision right then and there about whether to proceed, based on what you've just heard. Reasoning won't help you. It's just a question of listening to your gut and deciding whether you ought to trust this person. At such times, intuition is possibly more scientific than you think. Subconsciously, we all pick up subtle signs that the conscious mind isn't aware of, and they can signal when a person is lying. Perhaps we pick up a slight twitch or some other sign of nervousness, indicating deception. The wise negotiator knows not to ignore the signals.

Intuition can be thought of as a form of inner wisdom, and it is especially crucial at this stage of the negotiation. Discerning your needs, which have already been taken care of earlier, is mostly an analytical process. It's fairly clear what your needs are, it's not hard to articulate them, and they are black-and-white enough to quantify. Now, however, you're in the realm of wants, which are difficult, if not impossible, to quantify. This is where intuition can be extremely valuable.

Studies show that your subconscious operates ten times faster than your conscious mind. In a fast-paced bargaining session, the ability to quickly process tiny pieces of information can easily spell the difference between working out an average deal and coming up with a superb one. However, for your intuition to operate at this speed you must get your slow-moving consciousness out of the way by dropping down into the egoless state. Free of conventional thinking, the mind can instantly lead you to the answer you seek. This is especially important when you have to quickly decide when to hold tight to a demand and when to let it go. For example, if you've negotiated a good deal on the baby grand piano you've always wanted, would you kill the deal if you couldn't get the matching bench for free? This can be a tough call. A piano isn't just a musical instrument; it's also a piece of furniture that dominates a room. The piano might sound beautiful, but the wrong bench could ruin the look of your living room. You don't have all day to figure out what's most important to you. Intuition doesn't just inform you about other people; it can tell you a lot about yourself, too.

Sensitivity and intuition can be especially helpful during moments of confusion and heavy emotions. When a bargaining session is hot and heavy and both sides are fighting for what they want, it is easy for people to lose sight of themselves, and this renders them unable to ascertain whether their behavior is appropriate to the situation. One other benefit of intuition, then, is that it can warn you when you've crossed the line between aggressive bargaining and greed. Your conscious mind may not yet have detected what your subconscious mind already knows—that the reason the negotiation is headed south is not because of the other party. It's because you are being unreasonable and asking for too much. An old Chinese proverb says, "A man's greed is like a snake that wants to swallow an elephant." Many negotiations have choked to death because one of the parties just didn't know when to stop.

Free your intuition and you won't have to wonder if you're getting a good deal—you'll know it.

The Real Power of Silence

Silence is the true friend that never betrays.
—CONFUCIUS

We have seen how silence can be used as a tool, but now we turn it into magic. Silence holds particular significance in Asian culture. In fact, Asians are fond of saying, "An empty can makes the most noise," meaning that the person who knows the least often has the most to say—a message you don't want to convey in the midst of a negotiation. Indian mystics believe that silence is a relaxation of the mind and body, so it is restful as well as healing. It helps gain and preserve energy and vitality.

Many people, especially westerners, tend to be very uncomfortable with silences in the midst of conversations. They feel an intense need to fill in the gaps with chitchat. Asians tend to interpret a person's inability to shut up in one of three ways. First: "He isn't very smart, so he just has to keep talking all the time." Second: "His ego is so big that he just has to hear the sound of his own voice." Third: "He has something to hide." The final point is the worst. Many Asians believe that overly talkative people do this on purpose so the opposition won't have a moment's peace to think about what is being said. They think talking is being used as distracter, like a magician's sleight of hand.

Many Eastern religions say, "All new knowledge comes out of silence. Not from talking." Active silence means listening to another person without judgment, without worrying about what you are going to say next, but rather concentrating on what the other person is saying right now. You must also suspend your interpretation of what you *think* the person is saying and try to understand from that point of view. Putting your ego aside allows you to consider the other person's words as important as your own. The state of active silence gives you the curiosity to ask questions for mutual understanding, not just to meet your own needs. Active listening tells the other party that you are listening to be respectful, not to interrogate or accuse.

There are greater and lesser degrees of silence. On one level, there is merely an absence of sound. On a deeper level, you can hear the song of the universe. You might notice when you practice the meditation exercise that you become acutely aware of outside noises while you are sitting. This bothers many meditators because they say it disturbs their silence. It is not the sound of the car or the child playing that really bothers us, however. It is our own mind *paying attention* to those sounds. Real silence does not depend on the outside world, which is just following its own nature.

When we train ourselves to find true inner silence, the usual worries and distractions do not disturb us. Think of your mind as a pool of water. When a stick stirs it, the mud rises to the surface. Set down the stick and let the water become still. That is true silence.

TACTICS

Now that we have examined some of the advanced concepts that martial artists and negotiators alike use, we can move on to advanced tactics.

Using Silence to Your Advantage

It's a natural tendency for westerners to make an offer and expect an immediate response. When they don't get it, they jump in with a prompt such as "So what do *you* think?" If you're on the receiving end of this pressure to respond, don't give in. Simply look the other person in the eye with confidence; smile without saying a word. To novices, initially this seems a little too passive. "Shouldn't I be doing something more than this?" they ask. Actually, it is quite a proactive tactic because you are creating a vacuum that the other party can't stand and feels compelled to fill. The longer the silence goes on, the more discomfort the other person feels. This turns into a pressure to do something—anything—just to end the torture. Most people's response at this point is to give any perk to keep the talks moving. You didn't do anything. It was their own uneasiness that forced the move.

For instance, let's say you have a friend over to your house for a barbecue, and she comments on how much she likes your patio furniture. If you have been thinking about getting rid of it, you could let her know. Of course, she will ask how much you want for it. You remember that you got it on sale for half off and reply coyly, "I believe it retailed for eight hundred." She, being a sharp negotiator, will probably respond with something like "Would you take a hundred?" All you have to do is glance at her to show that you heard her and continue cooking the hamburgers. She is likely to follow up by saying, "How about two hundred?"

A variation on this *power pause* involves making a statement during a business presentation, letting the idea sink in, and then moving on with your talk. This pause adds emphasis to your words by giving people time to think about what you have said. If you rush on with your presentation, you lose the dramatic moment. For instance, you might say, "If we can come to an agreement in the next thirty minutes . . . I might be willing to include a free carrying case."

Again, probably nothing in your experience has prepared you to know how to use silence. Without training, you'll be just as uncomfortable with it as your opponent, so you'll be tempted to jump in and say something because you can't resist filling the void, either. Practice making statements and using a power pause before continuing. To really be good at this, you must prepare yourself to deal with the discomfort so you can just settle down and wait it out. If you need to alleviate some of the uneasiness of the silence, look down at your papers or periodically glance up at your opponent. In other words, occupy yourself so you don't feel the pressure of the silent gap.

The trick to dealing with silence is to learn how *not* to react. You can have any feeling you want, but just don't react. This is one of the most hidden secrets of winning a debate, a conflict, or a negotiation: the power of not reacting. It doesn't even occur to most people because their impulse to express their feelings is so strong. They don't realize how much ground they lose in doing so. They also aren't aware of how much trouble they cause in their lives by being reactive. Once you express yourself, that feeling is out there in the world causing a reaction of its own, and that creates one more thing you have to deal with. Practice being silent, and you'll find out how often you are better off saying nothing and waiting to see what happens.

Develop a Focused Mind

To become really proficient at defending themselves, martial artists learn how to develop a meditative focused state. Focus is simply the ability to control your own attention and not have it be subject to outside forces. It would seem as if tension and alertness would accompany self-defense, not being calm and quiet. Yet this egoless state—devoid of fear and other emotions—prevents fighters from being distracted by thoughts and lets them simply focus and react. Only in this state can they hit a target consistently. Normally, their egos would say, "Great shot." Once that happens, they have to stop and congratulate themselves. In that moment, they lose their concentration. In the next moment, they are ill prepared to execute another precise shot. The mind is getting in the way of the body's response.

As a master negotiator, you also can respond without thinking, but you must constantly practice the techniques in this book until they become second nature. It will be difficult at first because they are new to you. Like practicing any new skill, it is awkward and foreign at first. However, as you do it over and over, it will become a habit.

At certain levels of negotiation, you need the same acute ability to focus as a martial artist. At this stage of a bargaining session is one such level because people are more likely to lie. The stakes, after all, are higher now; people have more of a motive to hide their true intentions. As your opponent becomes more hidden, your skills of perception have to grow. And this is precisely what you can do in a state of ego silence because you are not distracted by words, facial expression, tone of voice, or anything else that could be misleading. One person can usually manipulate another fairly easily, but when you are above all that, you are not prone to ordinary methods of manipulation. You can see past all the opponent's deliberate distractions and remain unaffected. This gives you the power to stay focused on your own needs and wants. Your opponent's ability to manipulate you is his or her main weapon, and you have just disarmed it.

It is always critical for you to retain a clear picture of what is happening. Who wants what? Who is gaining the upper hand? Who has just slipped something into the deal unseen? Just assume all the time that your opponents are creating imaginary scenarios that benefit them and work against you. It is a given that they will try to accomplish this. If you are able to keep them from distorting your vision, you are way ahead of the game.

Beginning martial artists see a punch coming and say to themselves, "I must block it." It takes time for the thought to travel from the brain to the body. Masters, though, can see it coming and react without thinking or judging, and this greatly shortens their response time. We can see why animals react to the same stimulus so much faster than humans; they have no egos to get in the way of their response. They don't have to analyze the situation, make a decision, and then carry it out step-by-step.

Without the ego in the way, master martial artists can respond so fast that they seem to anticipate the punch before it is ever launched. Research has shown that egoless reactions are almost twice as fast as conscious ones. This is quite an advantage! Also, since they don't have to filter external stimuli through their ego, fighters can be even more acutely aware of their surroundings. The same advantage can be used by negotiators as well. Imagine being twice as fast as your opponent at the bargaining table!

When martial arts masters are in the egoless state, their identities disappear and they are no longer people but simply fighting machines. They have no thoughts, only instant and automatic reflex actions. All of their senses are open, so they can read body language cues, they can literally smell fear in the air, and they can hear what their opponents are thinking. The egoless state can also prevent a master's body from being drained by the effects of emotion or pain. Most amazingly, research shows that because masters have learned to slow their breathing and pulse, if they are wounded, there is less loss of blood.

Obviously, in most negotiating situations we don't need to be concerned about reducing blood loss, but all of the other benefits of being egoless can provide the same advantage over your opponent. The abilities to react instantly, have heightened sensory awareness, and even *smell* emotions are secret weapons that only a handful of negotiators in the world can claim. Don't worry; even though your ego is out of the way, your intellect is still functioning, in fact, to a much higher degree.

Active Rest

It is important in a negotiation to take a short break because it allows people to gather their thoughts and check their list of needs and wants to see how they're doing. In a bargaining session, though, it's important not to disrupt the flow—especially one that seems to be going your way. In other words, you cannot necessarily take a long break just because you need to, yet you cannot effectively negotiate on a continuous basis without some sort of mental break, either—especially after several hours straight. You will lose your ability to concentrate.

In martial arts we take what is called an *active rest*—that is, we focus on our breathing so that it appears we are not breathing. It allows us to reinvigorate ourselves without actually stopping the match. In a tournament you can actually rest while waiting for a response from your opponent. Eventually, though, you do have to take a real rest between rounds. Frankly, those scenes of Bruce Lee fighting continuously for five or six minutes are a movie fantasy. As someone who used to produce and direct martial arts movies, I know they are carefully choreographed and then edited together to look like continuous action, but they are actually separate scenes sometimes shot over a period of many days.

With time and experience, you will gain a sense of when you can afford to take a real break without disrupting the momentum. In the meantime, you need to take short but deliberate moments of active rest in order to stay sharp and focused. You can accomplish this by asking a question about an unimportant issue that doesn't require close attention. While the other person is talking, you can rest your mind. Try requesting a glass of water or say you have to use the bathroom. Do anything that lets you relax and pull your thoughts together and enables you to reflect on how you're doing.

In certain professions, practitioners must perfect the art of short yet invigorating breaks. Airline pilots, for instance, need to stretch their legs and relax their minds without letting the plane take a nosedive, so they simply activate the autopilot or have the copilot take over for a few minutes.

Control the Rhythm and Pace of the Contest

Every martial arts contest has its own rhythm and pace. So does every negotiation.

Rhythm involves cadence, tempo, flow, and symmetry. Martial artists use all of these when they are fighting. Initially, the rhythm of a fight is fairly even; one person makes a move, and the other responds in kind. As they warm up to each other, both fighters will generally begin using patterns that are more familiar. Fighter A might fall into a habit of doing two punches and then a kick, while Fighter B might jab, then follow up with a punch and then a kick. Once you recognize an established pattern, you can use that knowledge to score points. For instance, if you are in a match with Fighter A and you see his favorite set of moves coming, you are ready to block his two punches in a row and then counter before he can get his kick started. But this is also why it's important for *you* to vary your rhythm. The last thing you want is to become predictable to your opponent. Otherwise, he or she will catch on and use it against you.

All fighters have a rhythm they prefer, and it is often unique to them. And then, of course, when two fighters meet in a contest it creates a whole new rhythm. Fighters must be aware of the rhythm and make sure this is what they want. If not, they should try to change it to something more to their liking.

Cadence is, more or less, rhythm that is measured. Bruce Lee often said of it: "Speed, regulated to coincide with the adversary's, is known as cadence. It is the specific rhythm at which a succession of movements is executed." You must practice responding to an attack over and over again until your response becomes automatic. If you're not synchronized in practice with your partner, you could easily walk into a punch and get hurt. Bruce Lee called this "the art of rhythm."

Top martial artists are always supremely aware of the rhythm of a contest. It is just one more tool for scoring points. It is possible to strike with the beats, of course, but you can also strike between the beats, which is called being *antirhythmic*. It all amounts to finding a flow that's comfortable and establishing the right timing. At times a contest might be smooth and flowing, and at others it could be broken and choppy. One is not better than the other; each can have its own benefit and drawback, and you just need to be prepared to handle every type of situation.

Negotiations also have different rhythms at different points in the process. An offer is an offensive move (similar to a punch), just as a counteroffer is defensive (similar to a block). Sometimes a buyer will make an offer and the seller will make an immediate counteroffer. The buyer then rapidly responds by accepting some of the provisions while rejecting the others. This is a very staccato rhythm because each move follows rapidly in a different order. With other negotiations, there is more time between the beats, making their rhythm more regular.

Even if the other party in the negotiation has established a rhythm, you can choose to enter it and alter it with a change in tone. You might change a formal tone to a more informal one or use a joke to shift a serious mood to a lighter one.

Pace amounts to the speed at which a contest is conducted. Sometimes a martial arts contest is fast and furious, while other times it is slow and measured. In the opening round of the contest, the more experienced fighter usually tries to match the pace of the opponent until the fighter has a good sense of the opponent's capabilities and style. In the middle and final rounds, it's crucial to determine the speed of the contest itself because you want to fight your game, not the opponent's. Doing so will let you score more points, since you are working at a speed that comes naturally to you.

Like a martial arts match, negotiations have their own pace. They often start out slowly, as the parties get to know each other and each is trying to determine the other's position and style. Then, after the first offer is made, the pace usually quickens. That offer is the signal that the race has begun. As it is accepted, or when a counteroffer is made, the pace increases further. The negotiation can either reach a fever pitch if it keeps moving or bog down if the parties cannot find common ground. The pace can even grind to a complete stop if the talks hit an impasse.

Most negotiators have a pace at which they generally like to proceed in the bargaining process. It is determined by their internal speed, which tends to be based on their personalities. Type A negotiators usually do everything fast. They talk fast at the bargaining table, and when they leave to go to the vending machine they walk fast, and then they drink their sodas fast when they return. The only thing they don't do fast is sleep. These are the type of people who want to get to the bottom line quickly and get the whole process over with. Type B negotiators take a more leisurely approach to life as well as at the bargaining table. They are not in a hurry to finish or to leave. It can be quite difficult for two people who are stuck in one gear—first or fourth—to adjust to each other. The master negotiator is comfortable shifting gears smoothly from one speed to another.

Plan the End at the Beginning

Why should you plan the end before you ever get started? Because you should establish the goal firmly in your mind and work backward from the goal.

That is how you make sure you are always on track in pursuing this one goal. It's how you align your actions to meet all the specifics of that goal.

Not everyone can think well in reverse. The mind naturally works from beginning to end, not the other way around. If you want to work in reverse, you have to train yourself. And you must be in an egoless state because if you have a lot of distractions in your way, you can't possibly find the focus to accomplish this task. It's like trying to recite the alphabet backward. After a few seconds, if you aren't in complete control of your concentration, you will lose track of where you are.

Starting at the end point and moving backward to the start point is very challenging for the brain. Even in a simple deal, it is a complex mental process. If your mind is free, though, it will figure out how to accomplish this because there is a certain logic to a backward flow. It isn't quite as unnatural as it seems at first. In fact, we do it all the time subconsciously. Whenever you want something, that is the end goal. Right away, you're working backward from what you've already established that you want. An example is buying a mountain bike. Your mind starts racing. "How am I going to pay for it? How can I convince my wife to let me, a fifty-year-old man, buy a bicycle? What kind of bike should I get for the hills I'll be riding on?" A chart of this mental process looks something like this:

hills/type of bike/do research/what size/convince wife/money/***mountain bike***

In negotiating, however, reverse thinking is even more difficult because you're sitting right there at the table with someone. You don't have time to go off and make your calculations. And you don't have the mental space, either, because you have to keep listening to others who are there, to keep analyzing and assessing their position through their words and body language to see how the deal is going. You cannot afford to retreat into your own mind to form your backward strategy.

Needless to say, it is far better if you enter the negotiation having these calculations worked out in advance. Yet in any bargaining session, changes come up and you have to adapt. It doesn't matter how much you planned for a certain result, the other party has planned, too, and that person's plans have a habit of getting in the way of yours. To stay on track—to pay attention to the conversation in the room *and* the one in your head—you have to multitask. Here, you must trust your mind to come up with the right strategy.

Active Listening

We have discussed the art of listening in several places in this book. Now we consider it as an advanced tactic.

Most of us listen just well enough to know when the other person is about to finish a statement. Then we interject our own thoughts, which we've been formulating all the while the other person was talking. Basically, we blot out everything the other person said. The problem is that while we are thinking about what to say next we aren't listening to the opposing party, and in negotiation, that could be a big mistake. If you aren't hearing your opponent's points, you simply cannot keep track of how you are doing in the game.

Instead of simply not talking until it's our turn, we should pay close attention and listen, for three specific reasons: to verify, to reflect, and to clarify. As we said in Chapter 5, first you verify what you believe you heard to make sure you understood it the way it was meant. Essentially, you confirm that your understanding is on target, which greatly reduces future misunderstandings. Second, reflect to the other person verbally what you think he or she said, so there are no mistakes. This shows not only that you've been listening but that you empathize with your opponent's position. Finally, clarify your own understanding by asking the other party to expand on some specific idea or detail of the proposal. This saves time and frustration down the line.

So if a potential customer questions the price of your handcrafted wooden cabinets, you should first verify what her objection is to your asking price by saying something like "You don't think my cabinets are worth the price I am asking?" She might respond by saying, "Well, I've seen similar furniture in department stores for half the price." It could be that this customer just doesn't see the value of your cabinets. You could reflect to her by saying, "I know how you feel. In fact, I've felt the same way when buying a car. What I've found is that I'm willing to pay a little more for something that will last much longer. This ends up saving me money in the long run. Let me explain the difference between my cabinets and department store furniture." Once you finish your explanation, you can now ask a clarifying question such as

"So do you want a handcrafted cabinet or department store furniture? You know this is not a department store."

Never Split the Difference

In the middle of a negotiation it's very common for a novice bargainer to ask you to "split the difference." It sounds like such an easy solution that it makes some people feel it's petty to quibble with such a reasonable request. However reasonable it sounds, it is not a negotiating technique. It's just arithmetic.

Splitting the difference usually occurs when someone makes a ridiculous offer, and then when you object, the person says, "Well, let's split the difference then." In other words, we'll just cut my ridiculous offer in half, and then it will be fair. My answer to that is "Not so fast." The only thing good about this practice is that the math is easy—anyone can divide by two. But is that what you want the deciding factor to be? A number that is half of another number? What makes that fair or appropriate? There is no rhyme or reason to split the difference other than the fact that your offers happen to be apart by some number divisible by two.

If you're lucky, all this solution does is make one party unhappy—the one who is being asked to split the difference. Often, though, it makes both parties unhappy. Why? Because the buyer resents having to raise the price just to appease the seller, and the seller resents having to drop the price just to satisfy the buyer.

Smart negotiators never go for this tactic. Let's say you are applying for a job and research shows that with your qualifications, the least you should accept is $80,000 a year. Yet the employer offers you $50,000. When you object, the employer suggests splitting the difference, which leaves you $15,000 short of your goal. Why should you accept $65,000 a year for an $80,000 job just because it's simple to divide $30,000 by two? When someone asks you to do this, merely say, "I'm sorry I can't do that, but let me tell you what I can do. I can come down by this amount, but that's all I can afford to do." To sweeten the deal, you can also throw in some nonmonetary advantage to the other party that will make the person feel like a winner.

This is true negotiating because you are dealing with real numbers, not a fake concept. It makes both parties happy because the one proffering the deal is saving something and the one accepting made a concession he or she can live with.

Obviously, the tendency to split the difference is higher anytime you are $10, $100, $500, $1,000, or any even amount apart, just because it's easy math. Therefore, make sure that any counteroffer you make is not evenly divisible by two. For example, if the price of an item is $1,000, don't make an offer of $800, because there will be a tendency for the seller to compromise at $900. Instead, offer the seller $795. Not only does this figure suggest that you are getting close to your walkaway point because you've thrown out a number so precise that you must have carefully calculated it, but it keeps the seller from easily calculating a split-the-difference figure in his or her head.

Recognize the Impact of Cultural Differences

None of these advanced tactics work, of course, if you do not know how to read your opponent. An important extension of the subtleties of being able to read your opponent in a sophisticated way is to recognize that some people just don't think the same way you do at all. You may be reading other people by interpreting their behavior through the lens of what you would do if you were them. But what if they were raised with a completely different set of values, rules of etiquette, and way of socializing? If you don't grasp that there are fundamental differences and adjust to them, you might offend them without intending to. This would not start your negotiations off on a very positive note.

This gulf is never wider than when negotiating with people whose cultural background is different from your own. Keep in mind that any number of differences could impact the ultimate result of your negotiation. There can be variations in how you build rapport, establish eye contact, create physical space, or communicate—all of which can make or break your deal.

Building rapport begins with properly meeting and greeting the other party. Many westerners assume that shaking hands is automatic, but it is not by any means a congenial habit for everyone. As mentioned earlier, this kind of greeting is actually insulting to certain groups around the world, especially women from the Middle East, Japan, and India. It's better to hesitate for a moment and let your bargaining partner give you the greeting that is most comfortable for him or her and then just respond the same way.

Westerners also show a preference for certain habits. For instance, they tend toward very direct eye contact. In Asia, however, this practice is believed to be rude. To show others respect, people there look down when talking, yet this often makes many Americans and Europeans nervous. Westerners trust people who can look them in the eye and are suspicious of those who don't, almost believing that they have something to hide. Westerners must learn to get used to this tradition and avert their eyes appropriately when communicating.

In the West, people tend to stand about two feet apart after they finish shaking hands. This is approximately the amount of personal space they need in order to feel comfortable and not crowded. However, in other parts of the world this sense of space is not the same. In Japan, for example, people are much more formal and after shaking hands will step back to a more formal distance. Westerners who try to maintain a normal conversational distance will find themselves chasing Japanese people all over the place. There are, however, cultures that are used to much closer personal space. In the Middle East, for instance, people shake hands and then step in toward the other person so that they are just inches away. Westerners who step back to maintain the usual distance will find themselves relentlessly pursued by the other party.

Remember that communication styles vary around the world as well. Westerners prefer verbal communication almost exclusively, as evidenced in the school systems, where the common practice is delivering education in the form of lectures. However, in Latin countries people tend to be more kinesthetic, and hands-on exercises and projects are more the norm. When bargaining with Hispanics, use more demonstrations and interaction. In Asia, people lean more heavily on visual communication using charts, graphs, and pictures. When haggling with Asians, try to employ more visuals and do less talking.

You can see that these and other cultural differences can dramatically change the course of an intense personal interaction like negotiating. That is why I believe that my upcoming book on building business relationships with people from diverse cultures is so important. It has often been said that we are rapidly becoming a global society. Everyone has to learn to communicate with everyone else, and just knowing the language isn't enough. We have to understand and respect the whole culture, as well as the sensibilities of the people. Once offense has been taken, it is very hard to overcome it and start a negotiation at a positive level again. So when you spy on your opponents, include a little research about whether culture will have an impact and it will benefit you in the short and the long term.

It is so easy, when dealing with people from another culture, to assume they do things the same way you do. Half the time, we don't even stop to question because the behavior is so automatic. Stop and think first, and when in doubt, take your cues from the other person. Notice what makes the person comfortable and relaxed, and then follow suit. You'll find that your negotiations will go much more smoothly once you do so, and you will walk away with more closed deals.

Now that we've reviewed the advanced tactics, you can see that you have much work to do to actually implement them. Developing these skills requires practice and patience. Not everyone is ready for these techniques at this point, so you'll have to practice them as opportunities present themselves.

However, recognize that, as in martial arts, it is an honor just to be shown the secret techniques of the masters. Maintaining your honor in ancient Asia was a duty for everyone, from ordinary people to Samurai. It was more than just doing what was morally or ethically right; it required using power you had been given for good, not evil. If you lost your honor, the only way to regain it was by killing yourself in a ritualistic manner.

Although the concept of honor seems to have declined in importance in modern times, it is still alive and well, at least in martial arts and negotiating. As we've shown in this chapter, using the power of advanced tactics in bargaining is not just a question of skills but one of character. You can see that these tactics could be easily used for unethical purposes in the wrong hands. You are dutybound to use them in an honorable way. Otherwise, people might view you with distrust and even refuse to negotiate with you. May you always respect the power you have been given.

15

Breaking Impasses

To break an impasse one must be exceptionally creative.
SENSEI TABUCHI

In the East, there is a very ancient and well-known story of two masters who practiced the same style of martial arts. One day they decided to have a contest to see who was better at his craft. Word spread, and all the villagers in the area came out to witness what promised to be a spectacular event.

A ring was carefully laid out in the middle of town, with two of the top judges in the region chosen to referee the event and make sure the results were fair. Thousands of people poured in from everywhere and occupied every inch of ground that afforded a view of this historic event. Many of the witnesses had been students of one or the other of the teachers and were there to cheer on their respective sensei.

At the appointed time, the referees signaled the start of the contest, whereupon the two masters bowed to each other and then took their opening stances. They focused all their energy on each other with every fiber of their being ready to respond to any move their opponent might make. The two great fighters stood there mentally searching for an opening. They were both absolutely motionless for three minutes until the referees declared the contest a tie. This was the ultimate deadlock.

In a normal contest, a tie would go to sudden death. However, this was no ordinary match, and it was clear to all in attendance that the opponents were so equally skilled that no amount of fighting would have made a difference.

This is the quintessential example of a tie. A tie in a martial arts contest occurs when, at the end of three rounds, the judges rule that there is no clear winner. This is extremely disheartening to fighters because after all of this effort they are right back where they started.

It is the same in a negotiation. When you reach this point of impasse, it is absolutely disappointing. You started out excited and certain that the two of you could put a deal together. You seemed to be progressing for a while, and then the energy changed. In the East, they say that the ki has begun to turn negative, and everyone in the room can feel it. One of you actually starts to back away, but it's not a tactic. You aren't doing it to regroup or gather your thoughts, as you might have done previously. This time, you might really leave the bargaining table for good.

In a marriage, two people who are headed for divorce argue in a different way than people who are just angry at each other but are still committed. No longer are they offering any useful advice to keep the marriage together. They are only tearing it down, and in the back of everyone's mind it is conceivable that the union could very well fall apart. The air is charged. Just one wrong word could end it. The feeling is that both parties are pulling away from each other, and they want to be somewhere else because the atmosphere feels so negative. And they know that if they do walk out, there will be no coming back.

It is hard to tell when two people are facing a mere impasse and when the impasse has turned into a deadlock. According to my colleague, Roger Dawson, author of *Secrets of Power Negotiating*, an impasse is when talks become stalled over a single issue, whereas a deadlock occurs when the parties are negotiating but are not progressing toward an agreement.

In martial arts, an impasse exists when nothing you try seems to be working. In this case, black belts will reach into their bag of tricks for a secret hold or special punch to turn the tide in their favor. They may test their opponent by dropping their guard to see if their opponent tries to take advantage of it. You are not winning anyway, so this might be the time to try to be creative and different. You might change your stance, try a different style, or vary your pace. If you usually have your left foot back, put your right foot behind instead.

Fighters have to be willing to take chances at this point for one important reason: Whatever happens, you do not want to go into sudden death. Then you could lose to something that is out of your control—for example, a judging error or an injury. Black belts know that the longer an impasse continues, the greater the chances that a fluke could occur and circumstances, rather than skill, could dictate the outcome of the match. It is as if all the points you worked so hard to score earlier count for nothing. Now you have to start all over. Experienced fighters never want to leave a contest to chance because what would that say about all their training?

In a negotiation, an impasse occurs when an issue surfaces that stops progress toward agreement. You may have been putting it off, hoping it will go away. But it hasn't. At some point, all the other issues are resolved, and this is the only one left to talk about. You now realize that it's much thornier than either side previously thought. No one is budging. You are stuck, but at least you're still talking.

When the talking stops, however, it means you've reached an outright deadlock. At least one of you is probably about to leave. Perhaps leaving was mentioned earlier, but no one took it seriously. Now it is a distinct possibility. Everyone knows that you're both on a precipice and in danger of the talks completely falling apart.

Because there is a different tone in an impasse than there is in a deadlock, we will discuss each one separately. But first, I must point out that there isn't necessarily a direct correlation between a negotiation and a martial arts tournament regarding this subject. In a martial arts contest, the difference between an impasse and a deadlock is that the latter is more official than the former. The score is even, and the opponents are about to finish the final round without the score changing. A tie score isn't official yet because there's still time on the clock, but it doesn't look good. Somehow, nobody is going down. But when the time is up and it's still a tie, they officially move into a deadlock. In martial arts, a deadlock can only mean a sudden-death round in which anything can blow the contest wide open.

The difference between the preceding scenario and a negotiation is that in the latter, there is no judge and there is no official sudden-death round.

THE IMPASSE

There are a number of ways to break an impasse in negotiations. These are the most common:

1. *Change the subject.* Talk about something totally different; it doesn't matter what, as long as it's not the subject you're fighting over. If you

are in the middle of negotiating for a new car, for example, you might mention a movie you went to over the weekend. Everyone likes to talk about movies, whether they love them or hate them. All of a sudden, the tension lessens. Everyone's mind is off the roadblock, so space is made for creativity. Have you ever been faced with a daunting problem for which there seems to be no answer, and so you gave up and started doing something totally different? Then, suddenly, the solution popped into your head. That's the way this tactic works.

2. *Brainstorm together.* Say, "Look, we're so close. Isn't there anything you can think of?" The key to successful brainstorming is to come up with as many ideas as possible that could lead to a solution. Avoid categorizing the suggestions in any way because if you call an idea silly or unworkable, it tends to shut down future ideas. The most common negative response occurs when someone blurts out, "Oh, that will never work." Who wants to say anything else after that? It may surprise you to hear that doing the opposite is just as stifling. Don't say, "That's a great idea." Although this sounds like a compliment, what it really suggests is that all the previous possible solutions were inferior.

   To solve a problem, don't compliment or condemn. Just be neutral, because that is what keeps the ideas flowing. After each thought is expressed, simply get into the habit of saying, "That's an idea. What else can you think of?" When you dispense with judging, you generate more ideas. You are going for volume here because this is how you increase the chance that a true solution will be among the pack.

3. *Throw some wild and crazy idea on the table.* It may or may not directly lead to solving the problem, but it can lead to other ideas. For example, I was once negotiating a motion picture deal with a distributor, when we hit an impasse. The distributor jokingly suggested that he would throw in his rather mischievous teenage son if only I would agree to his terms. The mention of a child led me to think of schools, which then prompted me to ask him to give us the rights to the revenue from showing our film at universities. He agreed. Not only did this close the deal, it turned out to be very lucrative for us, since our film ended up being very popular with the college-age crowd.

4. *Change the form of the payment.* One of the most common impasses occurs when the parties become deadlocked over the price of some

product or service. The seller won't go down any further, and the buyer refuses to increase his or her offer. They harden their positions, and an impasse develops.

If price is the issue, which is not uncommon, the easiest way to move off it is to change the form in which the money changes hands. Instead of giving the other party the price he or she is asking for, try offering a larger deposit, increasing the individual payments, paying cash instead of using credit, or offering a higher advance. The sticker price is not always the most important issue. If it turns out that it is, and the other party is stuck on it, he or she can lose big-time.

5. *Handle the emotional subject of money as quickly as possible.* Otherwise, an impasse can easily turn into a deadlock. Money may not truly be the most important issue in a negotiation, but it is the one that causes the most impasses. Try to think of nonmonetary issues that could be used to sweeten the deal just enough to make it work.

6. *Change the members of the negotiating team.* Sometimes the problem is not issues but people. It becomes an ego battle between two personalities instead of a real bargaining session. Bear in mind that one of them might even be you. Bringing in your manager, a colleague, your spouse, or a good friend could eliminate the discord. Since you don't always know who is causing the problem, be sure to change all the parties, not just one person from each side. Retaining any of the original members could perpetuate the same limited thinking at the table. And take the time to bring the new people up to speed before letting them tackle the problem.

THE DEADLOCK

As we said earlier, a deadlock is an impasse that has turned deadly. The ship is going down, and all hands on deck are about to drown unless drastic measures are quickly taken.

If a martial arts tournament ends in a tie, it goes to a sudden-death round. Nothing in the past counts, and you must use your best technique if you want to win. Sudden death is a series of three-minute rounds. The person who scores first wins. It's that simple, and yet it is also tricky because you have to be aggressive enough to score but not so aggressive that you leave yourself wide open. In this case you must use what best fits the situation and your opponent. Newer fighters feel pressured to do something different. But this is a mistake because the new move may be less unfamiliar. They are not likely to execute it with as much skill. Even if the comfortable move doesn't seem particularly original, they should stick with it anyway.

Sudden death can cause novice martial artists to make mistakes because they're not used to the incredible pressure of this round. You simply cannot allow it to make you tense, no matter how much is at stake. Teachers will deliberately practice this scenario with their students, even though it rarely occurs, to acclimate them to that level of intensity. For example, Sensei Tabuchi routinely has his students spar using the rule that the first one to score is declared the winner. He doesn't want his students to find themselves in an actual tournament, facing this kind of stress for the first time in front of an audience.

In a bargaining session, if you can't break an impasse you will probably get only one more chance to make your deal because you are now deadlocked. Unfortunately, most white belts give up at times like this and let a negotiation die. They feel hopeless and think it can't be resolved. Sudden death is what separates the pros from the amateurs—black belts never give up, and great negotiators use this opportunity as a chance to shine.

When negotiations become deadlocked, there is a palpable feeling that everyone is giving up. The next step is walking away and taking the deal with them. Everyone knows it would take a miracle to turn things around. A deadlock of this magnitude must be dealt with promptly because allowing it to continue will stop the forward momentum completely. However, as we said before, in a negotiation, there is no official sudden-death round in which each side takes its best shots and a judge decides the victor.

When it comes to this point in a martial arts tournament, success usually boils down to conditioning. Less experienced fighters will fatigue first, and tiredness will cause them to make a mistake. Fatigue is more than a physical state. It is mental as well. Most martial artists have enough endurance to last more than three rounds. They are simply in good condition and can last as long as they have to. Well-conditioned bargainers are also in good shape. They are accustomed to long and drawn-out negotiations, so they don't grow tired or lose their attention when talks go on longer than expected. Fortunately, though, most negotiations don't last very long, so developing stamina isn't usually as crucial. Yet there are situations where this isn't the case. With government and union contracts, for example, negotiations can drag on for months or even years.

These are the most common causes of deadlocks:

- Both parties harden their positions.
- One party views the other's position as completely unreasonable.
- One or both parties become emotionally attached to an issue and cannot budge.
- Somebody pushes another's hot buttons, and the person suddenly becomes intractable.
- There is a fundamental lack of trust that the other person will deliver on the promises made.
- The other party cannot see any benefit in agreeing to your proposal.

If negotiations appear to be deadlocked, you should give it one last shot. Here are some last-ditch techniques that can lead to breakthrough:

- Come up with a concession that is cheap for you to give but valuable to the other party.
- Call a time-out. Don't let it go on so long that the parties just walk away.
- Ask the person who is taking an unreasonable position to come up with a solution of his or her own. Sometimes this can make the person realize how silly he or she has been. The person might even suggest a viable solution out of sheer desperation.
- Find a way to add humor to get people into a different mode of thinking.
- Break the problem into smaller pieces and deal with them individually.
- Introduce a deadline.
- Extend a deadline.
- Add new information that could be helpful.
- Change the spirit of negotiations from competition to collaboration.
- Ask the other party to explain his or her position and reasoning, if trust seems to be a problem.
- Educate the other party; understanding your position may soften his or her opposition.
- Get the other party to look at things from your perspective; seeing why you need a concession may evoke empathy from the person.
- Show the person the negative consequences of not reaching an agreement.

- Bring in a neutral mediator.
- Offer a choice of two solutions, which narrows the parameters. Sometimes too many choices can paralyze people.
- Go back to a point at which you were in agreement and start from there.
- Explore the reason behind the deadlock, not just the deadlock itself. It might be rooted in the past or some other issue. When the real issue is identified and dealt with, the deadlock might just disappear.
- Be sure you are trying to solve the real problem. Many times people propose solutions for which there is no problem.
- Watch the emotional level of the negotiations. A deadlock might just be the result of an emotional attachment to the item or the outcome.
- Help the other party save face—let the person look like a winner. In the Asian culture, saving face is crucial. If a warrior disgraced himself, he was required to kill himself by falling on his sword. Every culture has the concept of face; in the Western world we just call it respect.

This list explores individual options, but sometimes it takes more than one. When one tactic won't resolve an issue, a combination of two or more might provide the answer. Successful martial artists don't just excel at a single skill. They often put different skills together into winning combinations.

BE WILLING TO WALK AWAY

You'll notice that the one tactic not included in the list is simply walking away. Since there is a finality to this act, don't make the decision to do it lightly. You shouldn't really leave, of course, but you can use it as your last tactic when nothing else has worked. This dumps the responsibility to come up with a solution into the other party's lap. If the person doesn't respond, however, you must actually follow through with your move. There is no way to return to the table and show that you weren't serious.

The key to effectively walking away is to do it skillfully. You should not storm out and slam the door, figuratively speaking, which leaves you no way to return without sacrificing your dignity. Once you've decided to go, make sure you pack up your things slowly. As you're gathering your belongings, say how sorry you are that a deal can't be put together: "After all, we were so close. I guess you'll have to start all over again and look for another buyer." You're creating a sense of remorse that the other person just invested all this time and energy and now there will be no payoff. That very thought can make a lot of people modify their positions instantly. Once they do, it's a whole new ball game.

If you are a buyer, leave the door open to come back in the future with another offer. You never know—that could happen sooner than you think. At this point, one of two things will happen. Either the other party will stop you and reopen negotiations or they won't. If they don't stop you, you have definitely reached a deadlock. Just keep going and maybe you can approach them again with a different deal.

Don't insult the seller just because you're angry. Do not, for instance, tell a salesperson who wouldn't meet your price that the store lacks inventory. You never know; there could be other variables you're not taking into consideration. It would be awfully hard to return to this store if you burned your bridges during your last encounter.

If you are a seller, leave the door open for the buyer to end the talks without losing face. Then the person can come back again with a higher offer when he or she realizes it's not possible to do any better than this. Don't say what one real estate agent representing a seller said to me: "I'm insulted that you would bring us such a ridiculously low offer. You're wasting my time and my seller's time." Many brokers would have become so angry that they would refuse to work with this person again. Instead, I said, "I'm sorry you feel that way. My buyers believed they were making a serious offer on a property that has been sitting on the market for quite some time. I hope you'll be open to the possibility of us making another offer in the future if the property is still available."

Guess what? Three weeks later the property was still on the market, so I simply changed the date and made the same offer as before. This time, the listing agent was much more appreciative of our formerly "ridiculous" offer, which was eventually accepted. By allowing the other agent to save face and not becoming upset, my buyers got the home they wanted and the sellers sold their house.

It is important to be sure you are truly deadlocked by checking to see if you have first followed the rules of breaking a stalemate. If, however, you are truly deadlocked, there are limited options. Stall for time by taking a break and walking around for a few minutes. Or ask if you can use the bathroom. While in there, splash some water on your face as you try to think of possible solutions. Sometimes it helps improve your creativity just to get out of the same room you've been in for hours.

DEALING WITH ULTIMATUMS

One form of deadlock is the ultimatum. Many white belt negotiators commonly toss out the words "Take it or leave it" or "That's my final offer." Remember what happens when you push against another person's hand? The person instinctively pushes back. When you give an ultimatum, it probably won't have the effect you're looking for. The other party won't give in. Instead, the person will harden his or her position.

What novice bargainers don't realize is that an ultimatum is really a sign of weakness rather than strength. It basically says, "I'm out of ideas and too tired to be creative, so I hope this intractable language will force your hand."

There are four ways to deal with an ultimatum:

1. Call the bluff by doing what I described earlier: Pack up slowly and head for the door. In addition to saying what a shame it is that you can't close the deal, mention that you'll both be starting all over again. Of course, both of you already know this, but sometimes saying it out loud lets the reality seep in. Is this what you both want?

2. Go over the person's head by talking directly to the boss, broker, spouse, or a person in an equivalent position. Obviously, this might alienate the opposition, so you'd better be sure that whoever you go to is familiar with the deal and is very much in favor of it. There's no point in making this move if the new person is worse than the old.

3. Find a congenial way to let the other party modify his or her position by saying something like "I don't think you really meant take it or leave it. Why don't we try . . ." Most people who make an ultimatum regret it the moment it comes out of their mouth because it paints them into a corner.

4. Ignore the ultimatum. Just let it pass by, acting as if you didn't hear it. What I usually do is keep offering alternatives as if the other party had never said, "Take it or leave it." It is a gracious way to let the person take back his or her words without anyone making a big deal out of it.

5. Change the nature of the deal. All you have to do is broaden the project or reduce its size, change the quantities (more versus less), modify the quality levels, add more services or reduce them, extend or shorten delivery periods, lengthen or shorten the guarantee or service period, or the like. See if this changes the opposition's attitude. If it does, obviously the person's seemingly nonnegotiable position has now become negotiable again. Changing some of the details of the offer, then, is an easy way to test "take it or leave it." The key is to find a face-saving way by which the other party can retreat from this awkward position. If you can do this, the problem has a chance to evaporate. Most of the time, you've got nothing to lose by testing an ultimatum, so it's worth a try.

Remember, failure to agree is always an acceptable alternative to agreeing to fail, which is what a bad settlement spells for you. If you absolutely must make a deal, know that you will pay a high price for it. Otherwise, be willing to walk away at any point in the transaction.

RED BELT TEST

Now it's time to increase the difficulty of your negotiating experience by going to a flea market in your area. Every city and town has a place on the weekends where people sell their unwanted items.

The difference between a garage sale and a flea market is that most of the vendors at the market are pretty experienced negotiators, since many of them sell items at these events for a living. Use all of the same skills you used at the garage sales, and start bargaining. Then ask yourself these questions:

1. Did I create time pressure for the other party?
2. Did I notice who was under the most time pressure?
3. Did I test the deadline to see if it was real?
4. Was my mind laser-focused throughout the process?
5. Did I keep my ego out of the negotiations?
6. Did issues from the past come up for me? If so, which ones?
7. Did I use my intuition?
8. Did I use the power of silence effectively?
9. Did I take time to rest during the negotiation?
10. Did I try to deliberately control the rhythm of the contest to my advantage?
11. Did I plan the end at the beginning?
12. Did I employ active listening skills?
13. Did I refrain from splitting the difference?
14. Did I recognize the impact of cultural differences in this negotiation?
15. Did I see an impasse coming before it occurred?
16. Was I creative in trying to break the impasse?
17. Did I encourage the other party to be creative in breaking the impasse?
18. Did I encounter a deadlock or an ultimatum?
19. Did I deal with them appropriately?
20. Was I willing to walk away from the deal at any point?

If you didn't do as well as you would have liked, remember that there will probably be another flea market in a week or so. Keep practicing.

PART VI

Brown Belt

The tree is firmly rooted in the earth.

At this point, the negotiating knowledge readers have picked up isn't just rooted in the intellect. It is in the body. At the Brown Belt stage, you truly learn how to react with the instinctive intelligence, which is lightening fast. You hold in your hands the possibility of bringing the match to an end—in victory for yourself and honor to your opponent.

By the time the fighter achieves Brown Belt status, he knows how to uncover his opponent's weak spots. Consequently, at this point in a fight he can use that knowledge to strike at that weak spot when the opportunity presents itself. That is what Chapter 16—"Turning the Battle in Your Favor"—covers. Of course, a negotiator needs to be able to recognize a turning point when he sees one, that moment when the tide turns in favor of one person or another. Brown Belt martial artists can sense it coming and they have saved energy for this extra push. Bargainers can do the same. One who is experienced and perceptive can turn the momentum around, even when it seems decidedly against him.

Anyone who has been studying martial arts long enough to achieve a Brown Belt has encountered unfair fighters—people who want to win at any cost. In Chapter 17—"Dealing with Dirty Fighters"—readers will learn about the martial artist's code of honor, which is thousands of years old. Martial arts masters know, above all, never to turn their backs on someone who doesn't adhere to this code. In this chapter, negotiators will discover how to spot unfair tactics because, unfortunately, they are often disguised. They look and sound legitimate, but they aren't. Even a good fighter can lose if he doesn't know when he's being blindsided.

16

Turning the Battle in Your Favor

An alert warrior can snatch victory from the jaws of defeat.
SENSEI TABUCHI

In a martial arts tournament, the primary purpose is to uncover your opponent's weak spots, and to do this you use focus and concentration. Then, when the opportunity presents itself, you're in a position to attack without a second thought. This is known as *ma*—the moment in time that determines victory. In negotiating, this is known as the *turning point*.

WHAT IS THE TURNING POINT?

The turning point is a single moment that determines the success of either a martial arts tournament or a negotiation. It is that instant when you become aware of a definite change in direction; the contest is now heading to the end. Turning points raise the stakes, move the action in a different direction or to a different playing area, and force the parties to take a new approach.

In martial arts, fighters may discover that their opponents have suddenly become vulnerable to a punch or kick against which they had previously been guarded. In a negotiation, opponents might unexpectedly become attached to the outcome, and this hands you increased leverage. Or they may become anxious to conclude the talks just because a dealine is approaching.

In most contests, there usually does come a crucial point when the tide suddenly turns in the favor of one party and against the other. Martial arts masters sense it coming, and they save energy for that point because they know that when the momentum swings their way, they must be poised to take advantage of it instantly or the opportunity will be gone. Experienced negotiators can see it coming as well, and they're prepared to leap at the first glimpse of opportunity.

If, however, the contest is lopsided from the start, there generally is no turning point—not unless some kind of miracle takes place. You just know somewhere in the first rounds that defeat is inevitable and have probably decided to acquiesce to your opponent because, for one reason or another, you really want the deal. Either that or you decide you have to walk away from it. More commonly, though, players are fairly evenly matched in their power and leverage, and one small point of dissension can shift the balance of power one way or the other. When equals oppose each other, luck and timing play a more important determining role than skill or technique. You must always be ready to pounce when the time is right.

HOW FAR INTO THE PROCESS DOES THIS POINT OCCUR?

Although a turning point usually occurs in the third round of the contest, when the stakes are their highest, it can actually happen at any time, so you must be alert. In the first quarter of a football game, for example, an upset sometimes occurs when the home team fumbles on the opposing team's one yard line. The visitors pick up the ball and score, which breaks the home field advantage. Sometimes the home team never recovers from the turnover. In many football games, however, the score is in doubt until the last few minutes. One play can end it all.

If you want to detect and then profit from the turning point, you must have the patience to bide your time. For Asians, time is a weapon. They use it well by being tranquil and waiting for their moment to strike. How different this attitude is from the one in America, which has been a country for only about 230 years. Perhaps that's why we treat time as such a rare commodity instead of as a weapon. China, in contrast, has over 5,000 years of history. It's said that when Mao Tse-tung was asked in 1960 what he thought of the French Revolution of the 1700s, he said, "It is too soon to tell."

As mentioned earlier, I was once in Japan negotiating broadcast agreements for the televising of a worldwide soccer championship match. We spent the first two of our three weeks' stay with our Japanese hosts, touring Tokyo, eating sushi, and visiting karaoke bars. At the end of the second week we were growing quite anxious—and broke—because we were staying in very small but expensive hotel rooms. It wasn't until the last couple of days of our trip that our hosts seemed to feel comfortable enough with us to talk about business. They did not view the two weeks as wasted time but as a warming-up period. Fortunately, we did not lose our cool and misplay our hand.

Because time is money for many people in the West, we tend to be rather impatient. If you see this tendency in your opponent, you can use it to your advantage. By planning for the long-run, you can tire out the other side, and when they hit bottom, the momentum will shift in your favor.

Because the turning point may come at the beginning, in the middle, or toward the end of any contest, you must be alert as well as patient. There's an old saying that "a watched pot never boils," and the same is true for the turning point. If you keep waiting for it, you might miss other opportunities that come along. However, if you're alert and you manage to stay unruffled, you will feel the shift in the energy at the bargaining table, even though your mind has been open to everything else that's gone on.

You can create your own turning points. Whenever martial artists are up against stronger opponents, they can search for the opponents' weaknesses so they can strike at just the right instant, but they have to stall for enough time to uncover those weaknesses. Sometimes they will put their hands on their knees, pretending to be hurt, but they are actually using this posture to rest and increase their awareness. They may also bide their time by "throwing techniques" that do not consume a lot of energy, such as jabs and feints.

In negotiating, you can stall for time to gather your wits by asking innocuous questions or throwing out bogus offers. These could be noncommittal questions—for example, "If I doubled my order, how would it affect the pricing?" You are not *agreeing* to double your order, mind you; you're only asking. But it could send your counterparts to their calculators or even out of the room to consult their production department. In the meantime you can catch your breath and see if the tide turns.

Don't assume that there will always be a turning point in the final round. It's best not to wait until the end of the negotiation before taking your best

186 ··· BROWN BELT

shot. If you do it earlier, it might change the tone of the bargaining in your favor while you still have plenty of time to keep bargaining for more.

HOW DO YOU RECOGNIZE THE TURNING POINT?

How can you spot when the turning point is coming? Martial artists just feel the energy shift. If they're behind, all of a sudden there is a feeling of lightness as if a heavy weight has been lifted off their shoulders; they are able to fight with a renewed energy. In every one of the *Rocky* movies with Sylvester Stallone, he's always behind in the big match, but something happens to turn the tide in his favor. However, if you are ahead in points you might see the eye of the tiger start to creep back into your opponent because he or she really doesn't want to lose. You will have to summon all your strength to keep the pent-up fury from springing forth with full vigor.

Negotiators may feel that it's been an uphill battle from the start. Then all of a sudden the momentum seems to shift, and the boulder they've been pushing all day seems to have crested the hill and almost has an energy of its own. It no longer feels like such a great weight. This is no time to relax and enjoy the moment, however. The negotiators have to pounce while they still have the chance.

If things have been going your way all along and now the contest seems to be shifting against you, consider bringing the negotiations to a quick end while you still can. Once you lose traction, it is difficult to change the course of the contest again. And, of course, there may not be enough time.

Sometimes it seems like things are working in your favor, and all of a sudden you get a sinking feeling in the pit of your stomach for no reason at all. Pay attention to it because it is likely that, for some reason, the tide has begun to turn against you. You may not even know why, but that doesn't matter. What matters is that you understand what's happening. Try to turn the energy back in your direction, but if you can't, it may be best to cut your losses while you can.

To recognize the turning point, you must constantly be aware of the energy flow of the contest. Learn to feel the ki as it flows back and forth between the parties. With practice, you will become increasingly sensitive to this flow. At the beginning you'll just note it as an increased sense of enthusiasm or energy on your side or perhaps a loss of enthusiasm or energy by your opponent.

In order to see the turning point coming, martial artists practice something that Sensei Tabuchi calls *eight directional awareness*. You never want to be surprised, so you not only look to the front and the sides but also continually scan around and behind you.

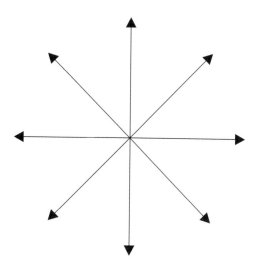

The key is not to be overly focused in one direction. Be ready to react to anything coming from any direction. Negotiators should not focus on a single issue to the exclusion of others because being myopic will make them miss out on other possibilities. Also, opponents can sneak up on them and ambush them and they will be too preoccupied to notice.

One of the signs that a turning point has occurred is that your opponent seems a little too happy with the agreement or is too eager to close the deal. He or she should be at least slightly reluctant to agree to a deal if you are doing as well as you think you are. Check your gut to see if a turn of events feels right to you. If not, stall for time to examine the situation. If you don't, you could regret it for a long time to come. Perhaps there was a turning point and you missed it. The deal is now strongly favoring your opponent. The other person knows it, and you don't.

The one requirement that is absolutely necessary for recognizing a turning point is that you have the right attitude. If you have a defeatist attitude, if you keep acting as if you've already been defeated, you will never see the turning point or the opportunity it represents. One of the tenets of Sensei Tabuchi's martial arts studio is to have an indomitable spirit. This means you never give up because you never know when your chance will come. Life is full of surprises. There is an old story about a man who had to appear before the king to answer for a crime of stealing. To distract the king from giving him a harsh punishment, he told his sovereign that he had a singing pig. The king perked up and was interested. He told the man to go and teach his pig a special song to amuse the court. He was to appear in one year's time and perform this song in front of everyone. If he failed to produce this miraculous pig, he would be hung. After he left the castle, his friend said to him, "So . . . what have you gained? Only a year. Then you'll be hanged anyway." The man replied, "Do not despair my friend. A lot can happen in one year. I could die anyway before then. Or the king could die. And who knows, maybe the pig will sing."

TAKING ADVANTAGE OF THE TURNING POINT IS ALL ABOUT TIMING

Timing is a process of regulating the negotiation to produce the most effective results for you. As we have said, it has always been important in the contest, but at the turning point it is absolutely crucial. To get the deal you want and not let the other party come out on top, you have to be acutely aware of timing. If the winds of change begin to blow into your face rather than at your back, you must make an adjustment before the momentum builds against you. The key to taking advantage of a turning point, then, is to master the art of timing. Your opponent may make a momentary mistake or a slip, and when he or she does, you must seize the opportunity almost without thinking. This is where training comes into play. Without it, you cannot respond instinctively, without thinking or hesitation.

Timing is doing the right thing at the right moment. You will know that your opponent is experiencing helplessness, for example, when you see a look of confusion or hesitation in his or her eyes, and that is the time to strike. When that juncture arrives, though, you must act decisively. As Bruce Lee has said, "The opportunity is there but only for an instant."

To respond appropriately to the turning point in a negotiation, you have to know when the timing is right to go after what you want. And to be perceptive enough to know when to take your shot, you have to find that opening. In negotiating, openings are created when your opponent grows frustrated or tired. This is where your conditioning and experience pay off. Once you have gone through a number of protracted bargaining sessions, you will have learned how to pace yourself. You have to rest along the way whenever you can so that when an opening appears, you can jump in with both feet. Of course, to create openings of your own, you must always be paying attention and identifying patterns, suggesting ideas, presenting proposals, making self-disclosures to build rapport, and paying compliments.

If you keep pushing, a deal will usually work itself out in your favor if you believe the turning point is coming. If it doesn't, you have given your best effort.

17

Dealing with Dirty Fighters

Dishonorable opponents do not deserve pity or compassion.
MICHAEL SOON LEE

Everyone wants to win, but you can carry that desire too far. In martial arts it's understood that all parties are aggressive and have a winning spirit, but without honor in how you play the game, the need to win can spin out of control and taint your victory. Every system of martial arts has its own code of honor. In their simplest form, these codes basically say, "I'm going to give you the best I have and will fight fair."

In ancient times, martial artists would exhibit this sentiment by extending their right hands and pulling back their sleeves to show they had no weapons—nothing up their sleeve, so to speak. This evolved later into the distinctly Asian practice of exchanging business cards with both hands for the same reason. It essentially says to the other party, "I have nothing to hide and I'm going to be fair."

THERE ARE UNFAIR FIGHTERS

Make no mistake, despite the martial artists' code of honor, which is thousands of years old, some fighters today are driven to win and will stop at nothing to accomplish that goal. Some use unapproved tactics; they hit you when you're not looking, or they sneak in a kick after the round is over. There are as many unfair tactics as there are unfair fighters. In a formal contest, a fighter can be disqualified for these lapses in moral judgment.

Once again, though, bargaining sessions usually don't have judges overseeing the proceedings. You pretty much have to look out for yourself. A negotiator must be alert to unethical tactics because when they're used against you, the only rule is that there are no rules. The only consequence for unfair negotiators is that if word gets out, most people just won't bother to bargain with them. And those who do sit at that table won't offer them the best deal because they figure unfair negotiators will cheat them anyway.

When martial artists encounter people who don't follow the code, they never turn their back on them. Furthermore, they are free to use similar tactics, when necessary, to defend themselves. Sometimes the martial arts community recognizes that a particular student simply will not uphold the honor of the group. In such a case, the teachers refuse to share their innermost secrets, and other students may refuse to fight that student. When unethical people are not taught secret tactics or techniques, eventually they find that they cannot win against more experienced and honorable opponents, even when they do resort to underhanded practices. In some situations, students may even be expelled from a school for a violation of its code of honor that is too reprehensible to tolerate. If teachers condone such behavior, it would turn into a cancer that would eat away at the moral fiber of the entire group. Nobody wants to lose, but there is no loss of face if it is borne with honor and if the fighters learn their lessons from it.

These are some of the unfair tactics that might be used in martial arts:

- Hitting an opponent after a round has ended
- Striking an opponent in an unapproved area such as the head, knees, or groin
- Using more force than is necessary to subdue an opponent
- Using weapons against an unarmed foe

Just as there are unfair fighters, there are unethical negotiators. Once people realize that certain negotiators are dishonest or use trickery, their credibility is usually ruined. Not only will others not trust them, but they might not even be asked to the bargaining table because people cannot believe that any agreement coming out of negotiations with them will be honored.

192 ··· BROWN BELT

These are just a few of the unfair negotiating tactics that might be used:

- Claiming, after the fact, that an agreement is not valid because the person didn't understand what he or she had agreed to
- Making an agreement and then trying to raise the price afterward by claiming that the manager "couldn't go that low"
- Using insults to try to goad people into accepting a deal
- Delaying tactics—for instance, sellers claiming that the product hasn't arrived, which gives them time to look for other buyers
- Arguing about whose position is more legitimate, rather than focusing on solutions
- Making personal attacks or threats to get the other person emotionally "hooked"

SPOTTING UNFAIR TACTICS

When you do encounter an unfair negotiator, first of all be very cautious. You never know what trick he or she will try and pull, and any agreement with him or her (yes, women can fight just as dirty as men) will probably not be honored.

Unfortunately, the only time you can spot an unfair tactic in martial arts is *after* it has been employed. Then, all you can do is make note of and watch for it again. Once in a while you will see a change in pattern or demeanor, which means that something tricky is about to occur, but people who make it a habit of doing these kinds of things are usually pretty good at disguising them. For pathological liars, there is no twinge of conscience. This doesn't bother them; it is just part of who they are. Prevarication is as natural for them as breathing.

In a negotiation, it's just as hard to spot tricky moves. They are designed to sneak up on you, but sometimes you can see them coming if you know what to look for. One of the most common signs is vague but palpable nonetheless: that something just doesn't make sense. The opposition, for example, suddenly seems to be stuck on a small, seemingly inconsequential issue, and you're wasting an awful lot of time on it—almost as if the other party doesn't want you to be looking in a different direction at other issues. Another sign might be an objection coming up out of the blue with absolutely no reason, which disguises the other party's true intentions.

In Chapter 9, you learned how to read your opponent, so you are in a better position than most to spot a ruse or a trap. If you see any indication that the person is lying, put your guard up. A little lie about one thing can be a predictor of more lies to come, because it demonstrates the willingness to be dishonest.

Ultimately, the best way to spot an unfair negotiating ploy is to listen to your intuition. If a deal sounds too good to be true, it probably is. If something feels wrong in your gut, stall for time to examine the agreement more closely or simply walk away.

COMMON UNETHICAL TACTICS

Once you have experienced unfair tactics, you will be able to recognize them the minute they are used again. Most professional negotiators agree that the following tactics are usually unethical.

The Good Guy/Bad Guy Routine

This is a rather sleazy tactic often seen on police television shows. Two cops are interrogating a person who's just been arrested. One officer is hostile, excessive, and even scary, while the other one appears reasonable and friendly and makes it look like he's on the suspect's side. The theory is that you will spill your guts to the good cop to avoid the threats of the bad cop.

Conniving negotiators use this tactic to hoodwink you into making concessions to please the person you like and appease the one you don't. The problem is, you are making concessions without getting any in return. If you find yourself in a good guy/bad guy situation, the best response is to ignore it. Recognize this game for what it is, but don't play along and don't allow the good cop to influence your decision any more than the bad cop does. The other way to deal with this negotiating ploy is to pretend to play along with the good cop. Go ahead and let him have his way, but not without getting what you want in return. If you are *his* buddy, he may feel obligated to make concessions to keep your "friendship."

Limited or No Authority

A person using this tactic tells you that she must obtain approval from an unseen higher authority before she can ratify any offer. This is most commonly employed in car sales. The salesperson says she must "run it by the manager," so she asks you to "make any offer" so she can take it to the higher authority. This forces you to make the first offer, and, as you'll remember, you can only go up from here. Of course, the manager always says your offer is too low; this way, they keep forcing you to raise your offer without the dealership having to give up anything.

Sometimes, this higher authority exists, but often your opponent will create this figure to gain an edge in the negotiation process by claiming there is a manager, when in actuality the opponent has the full authority to make the decision. Either way, it's unethical because the opponent gets you to put your cards face up on the table while he or she commits to nothing.

Another common example of the use of a higher authority is in salary negotiations. Your future boss might say, "I'd love to pay you the $50,000 you want, but human resources has a set salary scale and they won't let me go any higher than $45,000." This tactic takes away your ability to bargain because there is no one in the room to negotiate with—only some faceless department somewhere. This technique is designed to make you feel powerless, like a kid who has to ask his or her parents for permission for everything. The expectation is that once you feel this way, you will be more inclined to give in to the higher authority. However, just because your counterpart tells you, "It's out of my hands," don't automatically assume the person is being honest. In this situation, there are two options: Refuse to deal with anyone *except* the higher authority, or test the limits of your counterpart by asking the person to plead your case personally in front of the higher authority. You may find that although the other person is using this tactic to force you into backing down, if you persist, you can get the person to admit that he or she really does have the power to accept your offer. You can say, "I know a smart person like you certainly has the power to give us this one small concession."

The easiest way to beat the higher-authority tactic is to assert your authority from the beginning. I simply tell anyone who uses this against me, "I won't take 'no' from someone who can't say 'yes.' " In other words, if I can't negotiate directly with the decision maker, I will leave.

Another way to counter this tactic is to use the same thing against your opponent. Try responding to any offer by saying, "I have to check with *my* spouse (friend, CPA, etc.) before *I* can sign anything," and watch how fast your opponent's attitude changes.

The Red Herring

The name of this technique comes from foxhunting, where one unscrupulous team drags a smelly dead fish across the fox's path to throw another team's dogs off the scent. At the bargaining table, a red herring occurs when one side brings up some minor point to distract the other side from the main issue. This seemingly small issue then becomes a major point of contention for the other party. The intent is to get the person so engrossed in this discussion that the other party can sneak in other subjects that are much more important to them.

For example, I was negotiating the purchase of a house for a client. Everything was going along quite smoothly until the seller began to insist that the buyer promise to take care of the bird feeder on the front porch. I immediately thought this was odd, but I listened anyway. The seller was making all kinds of conditions, such as that the feeder had to be stocked with a specific kind of bird seed and that the former owner be allowed to inspect it at regular intervals. As we became bogged down further and further with the details, the seller slipped in the fact that the buyer should pay some of *his* closing costs. Recognizing a red herring when I saw one, I mentioned that the bird feeder seemed like just a distraction from the bigger issue of the closing costs. Once the tactic was identified out loud, we concluded the details of the home purchase without further interruption. Eventually we settled the deal: The buyer agreed to maintain the bird feeder but without any additional payments to the seller.

You can usually spot a red herring from the following moves: (1) Negotiations become bogged down over some minor issue; (2) your counterpart insists on settling this one thing before he or she will talk about the more important issues; (3) the other person suddenly slips in an unrelated issue; (4) the issue is inserted right in the middle of a discussion to which it has no relevance. If you recognize these four moves, it's probably the red herring trick, because most people are willing to put aside minor issues to focus on critical subjects. They certainly don't make them the center of attention when more important topics are still on the table. If they insist on talking about matters that amount to nothing after you have suggested setting them aside, something is fishy.

Bait and Switch

Bait and switch occurs when your opponent tries to divert your attention with an offer that seems attractive, when all the while he or she is really trying to get something else. The purpose of this tactic is to make you emotionally attached to one deal so that, if it becomes unavailable, you'll agree to a similar deal that is more advantageous to the other party.

This practice is very commonly used in real estate whereby a homebuyer makes an offer at or above the asking price but steals it back further on in the negotiation by asking the seller to pay for the buyer's closing costs, new carpet, loan points, or whatever. Another example is an advertisement that tries to lure you into the store by showcasing an item that is genuinely a great deal. Once you've driven to the store and your mouth is watering over the fabulous price, you find that the item is no longer available. The salesperson then tries to switch your attention to something else, which isn't on sale and is much more expensive. At this point, you've already wasted your afternoon driving to the store, and you've got your wallet out. You are in a spending mood, and you'd rather not go home empty-handed. Although it is unethical and often illegal, bait and switch is very common.

The Last-Minute Squeeze

Many negotiators know that when they're making a major purchase, they have the most power just before the product is delivered. That's when the seller has probably already spent the money from the transaction with you and has mentally moved on to the next deal. If you threaten to back out at the last moment, the seller will usually move heaven and earth to hold the deal together.

For homebuyers the moment of maximum vulnerability is just before escrow closes, for car purchasers it's just before signing the loan papers, for appliance buyers it's just before the delivery date is set, and so on. Some people will pounce on this particular moment to ask for a little more to sweeten their deal. A homebuyer might ask to keep the seller's power lawn mower. A car purchaser might ask for a free CD player. An appliance buyer might ask that an extended warranty be thrown in.

It is a wise negotiator who always saves something for the end of the process just in case the other party starts asking for extra goodies. If you don't, you may have to dig into your own pocket to hold the deal together.

The Emotional Hook

It's not uncommon for the person you are bargaining with to try to get you emotionally involved in the deal. He or she might literally call you names or insult your abilities as a negotiator. The purpose is to move you from the logical side of the brain to the emotional side, where you are more vulnerable and have less access to clarity and reasonable thinking.

Don't fall for this trick. Whatever the other party says, simply smile, breathe deeply, and recognize it for what it is. Then just ignore it. You also can try the old trick of counting to ten. Anything that gives you time to distance yourself from your emotions will help keep you on an even keel.

As mentioned in Chapter 12, if you let your opponent trigger your emotions, you are likely to lose the negotiation.

Nibbling

After a martial arts contest is over, some sore losers still want to continue the battle. They will hit you in the back after the final round has concluded or may even take the fight out to the parking lot. Most experienced fighters avoid such people at all costs. They have never entered into the true spirit of the battle, and they have no honor.

The correlation in negotiating is people who sign a contract or verbally agree to a deal and then try to change it. Asking for additional concessions after a contract has been signed is called *nibbling*.

This might be unethical in America, but you must understand that it may not be unethical in the country where the other party comes from. In

Canada, England, and the United States, when we sign a contract we assume that this ends all further negotiations. In fact, many of us believe that it is more than slightly shady to try to renegotiate a contract once it has been ratified. The common pronouncement on someone who is dissatisfied at this point is "You made your bed, so lie in it." However, in negotiating cultures, signing a contract implies, "I agree that this is what I'm interested in buying or selling. However, as we get to know each other over time, my needs may change, and I expect you to adjust the contract to meet those new needs." Nevertheless, these people also recognize that most westerners don't particularly enjoy haggling. They know that once a contract is ratified, we are generally so relieved and relaxed that we become vulnerable to nibbling. They may feel that it is perfectly within their rights to take advantage of that tendency.

Some people have theorized that many buyers who are recent immigrants ask for more concessions after a contract has been signed because they aren't sure about values outside their home country. For instance, the San Francisco Bay area has some of the most expensive real estate in the world; buyers coming from the Midwest often can't believe how much houses cost there. Imagine people from the Middle East and elsewhere who might never have owned a home before. You can see that they might think they are overpaying for a house here, so having a few additional perks thrown in helps to make them feel a little more comfortable about the purchase. It's almost as if they're saying, "I may have paid far more than I wanted for the house, but at least I protected myself by getting something extra."

From this explanation you can see that nibbling in negotiating cultures is not necessarily unethical; it's just a bargaining tactic. However, it can be very disconcerting for those who aren't used to this practice.

Many home builders I consult with complain that their recent-immigrant customers often want something extra just before close of escrow on a new house. I suggested to one builder that he try a new tactic: Don't include the free garage door opener as part of his incentive package at the beginning, but rather give it to the buyer as a closing gift. This way, he holds something out to pacify the nibblers. It's like saying, "I'm willing to give you an expensive garage door opener for free on the condition that there be no more haggling." All he is doing is changing the timing. Instead of giving the gift away sooner, he gives it away later. This tactic has since saved the builder tens of thousands of dollars a year.

Getting a little more than was originally bargained for becomes a source of pride for some people because it says that they are above-average negotiators. In real estate, I have seen buyers ask for additional concessions such as copper piping, the seller's furniture, new carpet, and even a rusty old lawn mower. They just seem to want to be able to brag to their friends, "Not only did I negotiate a good deal on the house, I also got such and such."

But why would sellers entertain the silly requests that accompany nibbling? In many cases, it's because the buyers are threatening to kill the deal if they don't get what they're asking for. It's simply a form of blackmail. Sure, the sellers could walk away. "But if it's such a small thing," their reasoning goes, "why not give it to them?" The alternative is a broken deal and a lot of wasted time. The problem though is this: If you do give them what they ask for, you are just priming them to ask for more.

So how do you stop people from nibbling? You could threaten to sue a buyer who keeps trying to change a contract, but that's a huge step and it's likely to have little effect on someone who comes from a less-advantaged country. In the United States a lawsuit takes about five years to actually get to trial, and in less industrialized countries it can take two to three times as long. Unless there's a lot at stake, don't even consider it.

One effective means to stop nibbling is not to pay for a product or service up front. Negotiate a payment plan whereby you give a good-faith deposit and pay the balance when the product has been delivered or the service has been rendered as promised. Then, if there is any nibbling, you have some power because you can threaten to withhold payment.

Another way to deter nibblers is to threaten not to recommend them to friends and family. Providing references is a powerful form of free advertising, and you can refuse the service if additional concessions are requested.

The easiest way to stop nibbling is to follow this one rule: Before you ever *give* a concession, *get* a concession. It's common for new-immigrant home-buyers to ask builders to throw in upgrades for free. I always suggest that before builders give it to them, they ask for their own concession in return. No exceptions. You never give anything away without getting something in return. When a nibbler realizes that every time he or she nibbles, the other party will ask for something, too, the nibbling will stop.

THE CODE OF HONOR

Every one of these unfair tactics violates a basic code of honor. There are codes of ethics in every discipline of every martial art, and yet there are always people who are willing to violate them because, for them, winning is more important than high standards and self-respect. Yet for most warriors, winning without honor is not winning at all. It is equally important to be ethical and follow the rules of honesty and fair play. For true warriors, honor amounts to more than merely playing by the rules. It is a way of life, an entire belief system.

As a result of its history, martial arts has become more than just a way to defend oneself; it is a journey down the three paths of life. First, it guides you to develop discipline and focus of mind; this is the mental path. Second, it leads you to build a healthy body through systematic training; this is the physical path. Third, it shows you how to display courage and caring even in defeat; this is the spiritual path.

The concept of honor in martial arts comes from the ancient Japanese Samurai code of conduct known as *bushido,* meaning "way of the warrior." It is as integral to the martial arts as physical training. The code stresses honor, self-discipline, bravery, refined manners, purity, and the warrior spirit. This code helps Samurai face danger because it removes the fear of death. Used as a tool, these traits drive out fear, unsteadiness, and, ultimately, mistakes that could get the warrior killed.

Of all the traits embodied by *bushido,* honor is probably the most central. A key component of honor is fairness, which simply means treating people as you would want to be treated. In the dojo it's not unusual that martial artists end up, at times, fighting less experienced opponents. The code of honor says that they must always spar with less experienced students as if they are only one level above them. Not only does this present senior students with more of a challenge, but it also helps them remember what they may have forgotten when they were at that level. The code dictates that no one will take advantage of those who are weaker. It builds trust among students, schools, and disciplines.

Being honorable at the negotiating table allows people to trust you. This makes the bargaining go more smoothly and, especially with complex transactions, means the deal is more likely to close. You can see that being honorable is part and parcel of becoming a black belt negotiator. Your reputation for upholding certain principles can give you power as a bargainer. Being known as honest and ethical will automatically lead people to be honest and ethical with you. If others know they are going to get a fair deal, it will make the proceedings go faster and you will be able to set up more deals in the future. Unless you never plan to enter a negotiation with them again, this last point should be very important to you.

BROWN BELT TEST

Find an antique store, collectible shop, or other retailer where the prices are generally flexible.

After you have completed your negotiation, rate yourself using the Belt Ranking Sheet in the appendix of this book. Ask yourself the following questions:

1. How did you rate?
2. What areas of negotiating did you excel at?
3. What areas of negotiating do you need to work on?
4. Did you notice a turning point in your negotiations?
5. Did you see the turning point coming?
6. Were there any unfair tactics used?
7. If unfair tactics were used, which ones did you recognize?
8. How did you deal with the unfair tactics?
9. Was there any nibbling?
10. How did you deal with nibbling?

Do not move on to the next chapter until you have at least achieved brown belt status on the Ranking Sheet. If necessary, find another place to negotiate, and work on your weak areas.

PART VII

Black Belt

The tree has reached maturity and has overcome the darkness.
It must now plant seeds for the future.

The color black is created when all the colors of the light spectrum have been absorbed into an object. That object has "taken control" of the colors and retained them. In the martial arts, the student has now mastered and taken control of most of the techniques and skills the master has taught. The only thing that now remains is to practice and refine them over time.

Winning a match might be the ultimate goal, but a master knows that it is important to win graciously. His whole attitude is reflected in the bow that occurs at the end of a tournament, which sends the message, "You were a worthy opponent." Chapter 18—"Ending the Contest with Respect"—is for the Black Belt negotiator who has achieved victory. If he wants the agreement to stick and he wants to do business with this person again, he must leave his opponent with his dignity.

As we see in the statement above, even the Black Belt is still on a journey of learning. The final chapter in this book—"The Road to Continuous Improvement"—is written for the Black Belt negotiator who wants to continue to refine his skills and possibly enter bigger venues of bargaining. It stresses the importance of practice to keep yourself in top form. There is not just one level of Black Belt—there are ten. To keep maturing, you must not miss out on any opportunity to keep up with your craft.

18

Ending the Contest with Respect

Ending a contest must be done with the same
forethought and planning as it began.
SENSEI TABUCHI

There is a specific ritual surrounding the ending of a martial arts tournament. Both parties bow to each other as if to say, "You were a worthy opponent." Then they turn and bow to the referee out of respect. In a match, there will always be a loser, so there will always be hard feelings of one sort or another. But this ritual is a way of wrapping up the proceedings so that everyone involved leaves with the sense of personal dignity, the feeling that the whole event was irreproachable and that is was worthwhile.

Ending a negotiation must be done in a thoughtful way as well—*if* you want your agreement to stick. When one party walks away feeling slighted, it affects you the same way an untreated wound does; it just festers and festers, and you feel increasingly worse as a constant reminder of its presence. Even if your counterpart had every intention in the world of honoring the agreement at the time of signing it, the residual soreness of a bad ending could cause the person to second-guess the decision. Even honorable people believe they are justified in going back on an agreement if they are drowning in resentment afterward. In their minds they go over and over the wrong they feel that was done to them—the insult, the shabby treatment, the imbalance of benefits in the contract.

If you doubt this tendency, consider this: Studies show that the risk of a doctor being sued has little to do with his or her competence or skills. Many of the doctors who get sued multiple times are actually very skilled, while many of those who make tons of mistakes never find themselves in court. How can this be? Because the decision to sue is based on how patients feel they were treated, not just on whether mistakes were made or even how disastrous the results of the mistakes were. The doctors who are sued the most consistently are the ones who talk down to their patients and are dismissive and uncaring. In other words, people sue doctors they don't like.

Opponents who leave the room feeling mistreated can easily come to the conclusion later that they are under no obligation to you at all because of how you behaved. This is just human nature, so why leave yourself open to it?

Always keep in mind that what people usually remember is the last minutes of the negotiation, not the first. Whatever emotional tone is set by the last tidbits of conversation or the final bargaining points, that is what you are both stuck with in the ensuing weeks and months. Make sure the tone is positive.

HOW DO YOU KNOW WHEN IT'S OVER?

In martial arts, either of the following two things will occur to signal the absolute end of the tournament: Time runs out or, in the case of sudden death, the referee clearly designates a winner. There's no doubt in the minds of the fighters or the audience that the contest is over.

However, in a negotiation the end is not always so clear. If you are working out the price of a product or service, it's as clear as a martial arts tournament; you are finished when both parties agree on a price. Simple. However, if you are negotiating a complex transaction like the purchase of a house, you must keep referring to the contract to see where remaining points of disagreement exist. The more possible combinations of offer and acceptance on various items there are, the more complicated the bargaining process is, and the less clear the ending point becomes. Having said that, if you see that all parties are fishing their car keys out of their pockets, if everyone looks satisfied and relieved, if they are calling their spouses and stuffing their briefcases, you can be pretty sure it's over.

Having a definite dealine for a negotiation, however, certainly makes the ending point much clearer in any situation.

DON'T TAKE IT ALL

One tactic that will definitely keep a negotiation from ending is when one party becomes greedy and keeps asking for more and more and more. This can really stretch out the haggling process. You think, after the tenth point, "Okay, we must be done now," but then you see the other party perusing his papers while he chews on his pencil, clearly regurgitating his thoughts. This can't be good. Here comes another demand. If you have this tendency yourself, just think about what it's like to be on the other end of it. You feel like you are the mark and the other person is the pickpocket who is there for the sole purpose of getting as much out of you as possible.

In the martial arts, the tendency to take advantage in this way is strongest when fighters are down or injured. Honorable fighters never hit opponents who cannot defend themselves. It isn't fair, and it creates a world of bad feelings, not just between the two opponents but in the audience as well. People come to see an honest contest, not a dirty, below-the-belt street fight. Disciplines like aikido make you responsible for your opponent's welfare, even if that person was the aggressor. This art is based upon the code of self-defense. You use only enough force to make it perfectly clear that to fight you is useless.

It may come as a surprise, but often it is the fighters who are way ahead in points who will end up losing the tournament. Why? Because they take some silly chance just to score a few extra points to make themselves look good. This is just another form of greed. Winning isn't enough. Fighters have to destroy the competition. Smart fighters who are ahead will not take any stupid chances. They hold on to the points they have and simply evade their opponents, letting them score only a few safe points. This makes the opponents feel good and may even cause them to slack off because even though they know they cannot win, they have nevertheless retained their dignity. In basketball games, you often see a team that is ahead *kill the clock* by lazily throwing the ball back and forth to their own team members and just letting the time run out. They could play a more aggressive game and score a few points, but then the opposition would have a greater chance of gaining possession of the ball. The coach also knows that somewhere down the road they may have to face this team again, and the situation might be reversed. When you're ahead, don't let it go to your head.

As we said, the urge to make your own victory bigger than it already is often occurs when your bargaining partner is in a desperate situation. But it bears saying again: It is better to leave opponents with some small victory and with their pride. Black belt negotiators always know when they have achieved their objectives. When you are bargaining, with every word you say you are revealing your true character. So think carefully about the kind of opinion you want people to walk away with. Being generous and exhibiting goodwill enhances your reputation for being a professional who doesn't have to play dirty to win. In other words, generosity and fairness broadcast strength. You are so skillful and competent that you don't have to be unscrupulous or greedy.

Both a sterling reputation and a good opinion from others can only help you in the future. Although you might think you'll never have to negotiate with this opponent ever again, you would be surprised at how quickly the tables can turn. As you've probably discovered by now, the world is a very small place indeed, and the marketplace is even smaller.

One thing many unethical negotiators forget is that if they humiliate others or take their dignity, those other people could still make it difficult for the negotiators after this particular transaction is over. Because "over" isn't always as final as they think. Say you have bought a piece of jewelry from someone, and you could smell her desperation for the cash, so you made her a take-it-or-leave-it offer that was far below market value. You pranced away, believing you did very well for yourself. A few days later, you realize that you need an appraisal on that necklace before you can insure it. She could make that very difficult for the appraiser if she won't provide you with its provenance. One way or another, you usually have to come face-to-face with the person sitting across from you at the bargaining table again, and if it isn't the same woman, it could be her uncle or cousin who has heard all about you.

If you are ever in doubt about how to conduct yourself in these situations, rest assured that the Golden Rule always applies. How would you want to be treated? Just answer that, and you'll know what to do.

ENDING THE CONTEST GRACEFULLY

Most white belt negotiators are so glad the bargaining process is over that they quickly shake hands, smile, and head for the exit. But this hurried departure leaves the other party wondering if he or she got such a good deal after all and may cause the person to try to renegotiate later. Resist the impulse to leave the other party quickly. It looks like you're trying to get away with something. Instead, take the time to end the bargaining session in a gracious matter.

The first thing to do at the conclusion is to congratulate the other party for having negotiated a good deal. Right away, this simple act makes the person feel good about having done business with you.

Second, point out the benefits of the deal as a reminder of why it's in the person's best interest to live up to his or her end of the bargain. For example, when I'm representing a home seller, I tell the agent for the buyers to remind them that they will no longer have to spend their weekends traipsing back and forth across town looking at houses. Now they can move on with their lives and spend weekends enjoying their new home. The buyers can stop paying off their landlord's mortgage and begin building equity in their own home. I point out all the little niceties of the house and how charming it will be when they have moved in and decorated it. With sellers, I gently remind them how peaceful life will be when they don't have to put up with strangers marching through their abode, touching their things, and invading their privacy.

Pointing out the benefits to the other parties in negotiations makes them feel like winners. It also keeps them from dwelling on what *you* got out of the deal and shifts them into thinking about what *they* got out of the deal, further ensuring that they will live up to their side of the agreement. Remember, opponents came to the bargaining table in the first place only because they had a problem to solve. They wouldn't have put themselves through the trouble of buying or selling otherwise. It's never hard for me to come up with the advantages for my opponents in closing the deal. I just put myself in their shoes.

It is also important, however, not just to bring up the advantages but to talk about the possibility of buyers' or sellers' remorse coming up. In the weeks that follow the conclusion of the negotiation, troubling thoughts are bound to arise in the other party's mind: "Did I do as well as I could have?" "When I had a chance to throw in those extra benefits, I think I blew it. I probably could have gotten more, but I wasn't thinking clearly." Monday-morning quarterbacking always places the negotiation in the worst possible light, because with the passage of time, we have the chance to imagine what a perfect deal *would have* looked like. But we couldn't live up to that because of the pressure of having to respond, in present time, to immediate inquiries and demands from our opponent. Now, upon reflection, we would like to take some of those decisions back if we could.

You aren't going to be there when these thoughts come up in your opponents, which means you can't answer their doubts and misgivings. And if you can't redress their issues, they're going to magnify until the other parties build up a case against the whole proceeding. You can prevent a significant amount of buyers' or sellers' remorse with a preemptive strike. Before leaving the bargaining session, mentally review the contract and the agreement and visualize any points of contention that might arise in the other party's mind. Answer those future objections then and there when you have the chance. I refer to this as "heading off trouble at the pass."

All too often, amateurs end contests without sufficient consideration. This is because they don't understand what an opportunity the negotiation's final moments present to create goodwill, to network and bond, and to cement a future relationship with their opponents.

19

The Road to
Continuous
Improvement

A true warrior continually strives to make his blade sharper.
ANCIENT SAMURAI SAYING

No one becomes a black belt in martial arts overnight. Each of the seven belts leading up to black generally takes six months to a year, or more, to earn, along with countless hours of practice to master the various new techniques and take the tests required to pass each level. In addition, you will be sparring with partners and taking part in occasional tournaments. So martial artists practice constantly. Whether it's punching or kicking a bag, sparring, or, participating in tournaments, they know that practice is essential to hone and perfect their skills. Even a teacher's study is never done. Instructors are always learning new techniques, reading magazines and books, and talking to other teachers just to stay ahead of their students.

The parallel to becoming a world-class negotiator is clear. You can't transform yourself into one without a lot of preparation and practice. Top negotiators are always looking for opportunities to practice their skills, to read books and articles on the subject, and to talk to others about new techniques. They relish the chance to try different tactics before they might actually have to use them. But to begin with, you must practice in low-risk venues so that you don't have to worry about emptying out your bank account just to gain experience. The main advantage of small, incremental risks is the confidence they provide. It gives you the necessary foundation for being decisive so that when a real opportunity presents itself you will be able to commit to a move instantly. If you don't leap at the right moment, you will see how quickly the opportunity vanishes. As Jennifer Lawler says in her book *Dojo Wisdom,* "To jump, both feet must leave the ground." In other words, if you hold back at all, you cannot take action.

PARTING TIPS

The following, then, are the final tips for becoming a black belt negotiator.

1. Learn the Basics

Go back over the basic rules of negotiating before you venture out into the cold, cruel world. This will give you a tremendous advantage when bargaining, because few westerners have taken a class or even read a book on negotiating. Why should they bother when they haggle so rarely? However, now you know better and can use this knowledge to your advantage every single day.

2. Start Small

As mentioned, a great place to practice your negotiating skills is at garage sales. For less than $20, you are presented with the opportunity to bargain for several hours. Remember science classes in school? Think of this as lab time. Garage sales are what I call a *low-risk venue* because the stakes are low but the skills you learn are the same as those used in million-dollar transactions.

At the sale, remember to apply the principles you learned previously in this book. To begin with, do your homework by looking in the weekend edition of your local newspaper. You'll find dozens if not hundreds of yard sales advertised. Some ads may even list the major items for sale—furniture, housewares, baby clothes, office equipment, and so on. If you see many ads for similar goods, you know that these items ought to be more negotiable than those that are less widely available.

In this risk-free venue, you can afford to be fearless. I know it's an odd thing to say, but I was lucky because when I was young I was very sick. Once I recovered, I found that there were few things that I truly feared because I had survived death. Anything else was only a small bump in the road compared to what I had been through. Better to start small, though, than to wait for a catastrophic event to eliminate your fear.

3. Do Your Homework

Pick a garage sale that strikes your fancy, then go look at what is for sale. When you get there, remember to check out everything being offered to determine whether there is something you are truly interested in. If not, don't waste time; move on to another sale. Once you have found something you really like, continue your research by talking to the seller. You can gather valuable information simply by asking a few questions, like these:

- "Why are you having a garage sale?" This tells you how flexible the seller's prices will be. A seller who is trying to make space in the garage to park the car is likely to be very open to negotiating. This seller is looking for space, not money. However, a seller who is raising funds to send the kids to private school may consider price as more important.
- "How many people have come by so far today?" If a lot of people are attracted to this sale, you will have more competition than you would somewhere else. Be prepared to pay a higher price here than elsewhere.
- "Is this your first garage sale?" Novices often have an exaggerated opinion of what their junk is worth, so you have to consider whether trying to educate them is worth your time. Those with greater experience will likely be more realistic, so you might actually get a better deal with less haggling.
- "What time do you plan to close today?" As always, people are likely to make larger concessions as the dealine approaches. After all, do they really want to have to try to sell this stuff the next day or haul it off to the local thrift store or junkyard?

- "Will you be holding another garage sale soon?" People who are planning another sale in the near future will probably just keep any unsold items rather than selling them off at bargain prices. This gives you less leverage.

4. Identify Vital Striking Points

After setting your sights on one or two items, note how much attention is being paid to them by other shoppers. Then step back and just observe the traffic flow. How much interest do other people show in the goods for sale? Obviously, the more competition there is for the items you want, the less open to negotiating the seller will be. Does the seller seem emotionally attached to any one item or another? Does he or she appear anxious to get rid of the stuff? Stand close as the seller talks to other shoppers so you can overhear whether he or she is making deep discounts from the marked prices.

5. Show Interest in an Item You Don't Really Want

Pick an item of similar *value* to the one you would like to buy, but one you do *not* actually want to buy. This might seem like a waste of time, but, trust me, it's really not. You're using a "decoy" to help you figure out the seller's negotiating style, how flexible the price is, and many other valuable pieces of information, without giving away your true position. It also enables you to find out the seller's true bottom line and then walk away without any hesitation, because you didn't want this item in the first place. But the message you're sending the seller is that you are not the type of person to grow emotionally attached, so he or she can't strong-arm you into buying or be inflexible.

6. Get the Other Party to Commit First

Begin to bargain for one of the items you really don't care about. You might open with a question like this: "I see the price marked here, but, seriously, how much would you really take?" Whatever price the seller quotes you, remember to flinch and then watch for the person's reaction. If the seller does not lower the price further at that point, try responding, "Well I was thinking more of [pick a figure that is half of whatever you were quoted]." The seller's next response will tell you how flexible the price is.

7. Find Middle Ground

Find middle ground by bargaining back and forth. The objective here is to see how negotiable the seller is on the item you *aren't* interested in. You will also get a sense of the person's negotiating style and experience. Take your time and observe closely. How does the person react to low offers? How fast does he or she drop the price? How far does he or she drop the price?

Where is the middle ground, where you are happy with the deal and the other party is satisfied with what he or she is receiving as well? This is where you want to spend the bulk of your time and energy.

8. Create Time Pressure

Let the seller know that you plan to look at similar items at other garage or yard sales. In other words, the seller's competition is the entire neighborhood. Be sure to note how he or she reacts to this statement. Someone who seems to grow more intense is sensitive to the time pressure created by the possibility that you will leave and won't return. You can use this as leverage to build a better deal for yourself. If the seller appears to be indifferent to time pressure, don't expect to do much better by sticking around.

9. Use the Knowledge You've Gained So Far

Finally, move to the item you really want and begin the bargaining process in earnest, now knowing how negotiable you should expect the seller to be on your item. Your earlier practice should save you time and help you purchase at a bargain price because you now know the seller's tactics and you've probably worn him or her down a bit.

10. Be Willing to Walk Away

If the seller won't accept the price you want, you can always come back toward the end of the day and see whether your item is still available. If it is, you can then use the power of the dealine to leverage the best deal possible. Remember to point out the fact that the seller doesn't want to have to store it for another week or even end up just taking it to the dump.

PRACTICE, PRACTICE, PRACTICE

Just like any skill, negotiating must be constantly drilled into your mind. The ultimate place to build experience, besides garage sales, is at your local flea market. Most of these venues are large, open-air arenas that feature everything from brand-new tires to electronics and rare books. If you can't find something you could use at a flea market, you're just not trying. In addition, the sellers are usually fairly sophisticated at negotiating, having done it week after week, possibly for years. You are sure to pick up valuable experience from them if you observe carefully. Just remember to follow the tactics you've already learned. If you keep going to these places, you will most certainly improve your skills.

Garage sales and flea markets are by no means the only places to hone your haggling technique. Every time you are about to reach into your wallet, ask yourself whether this might be an opportunity to bargain. The goal is to start bartering for nearly everything you buy. Yes, this takes time, but so does becoming a black belt in martial arts. Moving up in the ranking to black belt is a long process. Generally, to earn a first-degree black belt takes a year. To earn a second-degree black belt takes two years, a third-degree is three years, and so on. You can see that to earn a tenth-degree black belt takes quite a few years, not including all the time it took to earn the belts leading up to the black belt. It's an investment in a skill that pays big dividends over time in terms of increased health, discipline, and focus that can be applied to other areas of life. You'll find many top salespeople, managers, CEOs, ministers, and others who attribute their success to the study of martial arts.

Just as martial artists need to spar, negotiators must practice their own form of sparring. Try to think of all the places you could practice your negotiating skills. And don't forget that more items in this world are negotiable than you think.

Practicing your bargaining skills is essential to eliminating fear. Bruce Lee was fond of saying, "Frequent encounters with fear make you strong." The reason is that being afraid is no longer an unfamiliar experience that throws you off balance and interferes with your ability to think strategically. After a while, the fear appears, but it quickly recedes into the background. It doesn't make you squeamish. It doesn't make you want to run away. It certainly doesn't make you back down. Once you learn to control your fear, you can stand up to anyone, and in a negotiation, that is what it often boils down to. As in a poker game, the key to success is this: Just don't blink.

Remember: Every time you have to pay for a product or service, ask yourself whether this is an opportunity to negotiate. White and yellow belts should literally put a note in their wallets to remind them to think about winning a discount on every purchase. I'm not saying you *need* to bargain for every little item; it may not be worth the effort. However, you must get into the habit of at least thinking about the possibility of haggling rather than just automatically paying full price.

One example that comes to mind is the day I was contacted by a major association to feature our company in its upcoming directory, which advertises multicultural researchers. Each ad cost $275. Research is only a small part of the services my company provides; it is far more focused on consulting with companies to teach their salespeople to be culturally competent and negotiate effectively. When I explained this to the association's representative, she told me that perhaps I would be more interested in a spot in the consultants' directory, which would be out in a few months. I immediately thought of advertising in both issues and asked if there would be a price break for two. She responded yes, the price would drop to $200 *per* directory. Right away, I saved $150 per issue, and it didn't take much effort. Then I reminded her that this was my company's first time advertising with this association. We didn't even know yet if it would provide enough response from readers to make it worthwhile. Could she do any better on the two-issue package until we saw whether it would pay off? Again she dropped the price, this time to $175 for each issue. Now we were saving $200. Not a bad discount for ten-minutes' work. That's the equivalent of earning $1,200 an hour!

What was the worst thing that could have happened if I had asked for a discount and the representative had said no? I probably would have advertised only in the consultants' directory, and the association would have lost $125 in revenue. Instead, they got $350 in total income, and we got two issues in which to test our marketing. Although I believe we got the better end of the deal, we both ultimately got what we wanted.

I know many people who would have let a chance like this go by without testing the water. Think back over your own last week by using your calendar to jog your memory. How many opportunities did you have to negotiate? None? I doubt it.

Besides advertising, another item people often point to as nonnegotiable is food. Frankly, you are not likely to obtain a discount on your weekly grocery because the profit margin on food is very low—only 2 to 3 percent. However, there are other areas to be considered. The local school my son attends wanted to buy snacks and other items to resell to the students to raise money. So I negotiated with the distributor for a 60 percent discount off potato chips and cookies for bulk purchases. I did the same thing when the school wanted fruits and vegetables for the cafeteria.

Now, if you want to go to the trouble of putting together a buying group from among your friends and neighbors, I'm sure you could arrange a substantial discount on large food purchases from your local market. Would it be worth the time and effort? Only if the discount you receive is high relative to the amount of time you have to invest.

The final item that people hold up as being absolutely nonnegotiable is medical care. You must remember that the law of supply and demand dictates that the more demand there is for an item, the higher its price. Converting this rule into negotiating terms means that the more competition there is, the lower the discount you will be able to negotiate. But if you have built up a long-term relationship with your physician or dentist, and they know you've been referring others to them for years, you certainly have acquired a certain amount of goodwill. Consider leveraging that into a price reduction. We always get a 10 percent courtesy discount from our dentist because we refer so much business to him.

Think about your life. Did an advertiser call, asking you to place an ad in the Yellow Pages, in a directory, or in the local newspaper? Did you go to dinner at a restaurant that you often frequent? Is there a sandwich shop you visit on a regular basis? Did you buy office supplies from a stationery store? Did you take your clothes to the local dry cleaner? Do you pay an annual fee on your credit card? Is your credit card interest rate too high? All of these, and more, were opportunities to practice your negotiating skills, and you probably missed them.

When you first start doing this, you will feel like a white belt, I promise you. But after a while, many of the principles in this book will become second nature, and you'll be bargaining like a pro in no time. You will feel yourself moving up the ranks of negotiators. Use the Belt Ranking Sheet in the appendix of this book to track your progress and make notes for improvement.

TO GET OUT OF YOUR COMFORT ZONE, GET OUT OF THE COUNTRY

If you have the chance to travel to other countries to watch people bargain every day, I hope you take advantage of it. First, you'll gain a greater appreciation for your home country because one of the reasons people negotiate so hard in many of these places is that they have to; they are very poor, and money is in short supply. For them, getting a vendor to cut a price could mean more than just getting a good deal—it could mean survival.

Second, you will pick up tips on bargaining from some of the best negotiators in the world because they've been doing it since they were kids. I have bargained for carpets in Turkey, for statues in Mexico, for cabs in Greece, for tours in Rome, for jade pendants in China, for pearl necklaces in Japan, for watches in St. Maarten, and more. Each culture has a different style of negotiating, and all have given me skills to barter more skillfully in various situations. You just never know when the aggressive style of the Greeks might be blended with the more reserved style of the Japanese to put together a fabulous deal.

The martial arts sometimes hold contests in which various styles, not just one, are used, and both the practitioners and the audience pick up valuable skills. For example, a karate student might gain knowledge about throwing an opponent from a judo fighter, about grappling from a wrestler, or even about balance from a tai chi student. You never know when one of these skills will come in handy to win a tournament or save your life.

Martial artists cross-train using a variety of techniques and weapons, so they don't have to rely on just one. Negotiators must cross-train in different venues to increase their flexibility. This is why you should not only look for opportunities to negotiate but search out various kinds of opportunities—products, services, low-priced items, high-priced items—when you bargain. Very often you will come across some unusual and rather esoteric techniques that don't seem to apply to your usual negotiating opportunities, and at first, they may seem useless.

Of course, the Chinese have a proverb for this as well: "Useless knowledge may have hidden uses." In martial arts, we practice many moves that seem, in the beginning, to have no practical use. Star pupils do them without question, but marginal practitioners question the need for them. For example, in the movie *The Karate Kid*, the master has the student practicing "wax on/wax off" motions while polishing his car. Believing that the teacher is only using him to shine his car, the pupil rebels. Then the teacher points out the real lesson: Constantly repeating these seemingly purposeless moves is actually teaching him how to instinctively block a punch.

I have found myself in many situations where, at first, I felt like a fish out of water. I had no idea how to bargain for what I wanted because I had never been in this position before. When producing a low-budget motion picture, I wanted to preserve our budget for anything that had real screen value. Unfortunately, behind-the-scenes costs—equipment rental, studio lights, trailers for actors' dressing rooms, and beer for the crew—were consuming the bulk of the film budget. None of these made our film look like a big-budget movie. Consequently, I had to spend a great deal of time obtaining most of these items for free, so I could put the bulk of the money where it really counted. This haggling was unlike anything else in the world, and yet daily I found myself using some of the same techniques I employed in my everyday life. Getting a discount on something as ordinary as sandwiches from my local deli is not much different from getting a restaurant to give our entire crew free lunches for a month in exchange for free publicity in the film.

When sparring in the dojo, martial artists and their partners are learning from each other all the time. In the same way, you and the person sitting on the other side of the bargaining table are also learning from each other. So whether you find yourself in a foreign country or in a foreign situation right here at home, make use of every opportunity to improve your negotiating skills by watching those around you.

HOW TO PRACTICE

Even when they're alone, martial artists practice just to challenge themselves. They perform what we call *katas*. Katas are dances with very precise and set moves that let students practice kicks, punches, blocks, turns, and techniques. This is the equivalent of shadowboxing for prizefighters, except that the order of attacks by your opponent are predetermined.

When you are practicing in the dojo there are different levels of contact—no-contact, light-contact, and full-contact sparring. In no-contact sparring, you hit close to your opponent, but you don't actually strike the person. Perhaps your kick is close enough that your opponent can even feel the air being displaced by your foot. To score, the strike must be so near that the judges can tell that you *could* have made contact if you had wanted to. In negotiating, of course, it is quite difficult to "spar" by yourself, but there are things you can do on your own to prepare. You can practice in front of a mirror. Try out a few flinches, for example, and see if they are convincing. On your own, you can also research the product or service you want to buy or the market in which the bargaining will take place. Any preliminary preparation can be done solo, including reading this book.

Light-contact sparring gives the martial artist a sense of what it's like to be in a real fight but in a safe environment. Although you are allowed to hit your partner, it can only be a light tap. You're just getting a sense of what kind of shape you're in and how well your technique works. And just as cars have air bags in case of an accident, fighters wear protective headgear. At the beginning of this chapter, I advocated going to a lot of flea markets and garage sales to practice your craft. This is analogous to light-contact sparring. You have the chance to experience the bargaining process in a relatively safe venue.

Full-contact sparring is a knockdown, drag-out fight. Your only protection is the rules of the game. (Unfair techniques such as biting and striking in the groin are strictly forbidden.) Your partner is really trying to hit you, and when he does, you will feel it. People can and do get hurt. In other words, the fighters have something to lose, so they had better know what they're doing. The equivalent in negotiating is when people are bargaining over a high-ticket item, and if they don't come out the winner, they could lose a great deal of money. The most common high-ticket items are cars and homes. As the old saying goes, "Don't try this one at home." In other words, do not walk into a

222 --- BLACK BELT

high-stakes negotiation by yourself unless you have quite a bit of experience under your belt and you know how to play the game with other experienced players.

DISCIPLINE AND BALANCE

There are many more white belts than brown or black belts because quite a few of the people who begin their studies lack the discipline to continue. They often realize that they don't want to go through all of the training and practice that it takes to be superior at it. Some quit after they lose one tournament. Great fighters consider a loss to be just another lesson.

Aspiring black belt negotiators have the same mentality. For instance, they must have the discipline to practice regularly by blocking out dates on their calendar when they're going to visit garage sales, flea markets, antique stores, collectible shops, consignment centers, and so on. Then they tell their spouse or friends about it so they can be held accountable for completing their mission. Then your family or friends will ask you how it went after you were supposed to go. This may not sound like much, but you would be surprised how much more disciplined people are about following through on a promise when they make it to someone other than just themselves. We might be willing to let ourselves down, but we don't usually want others to think of us as slackers.

Another way to become proficient at negotiating is to pass on to others what you have learned in this book. Whenever you have to teach an idea to someone else, you really have to figure out what you know. You have to think about it or you can't articulate it. By helping friends and family become better bargainers, you'll find that the principles of black belt negotiating become more ingrained in your mind.

Balance is another critical tenet of martial arts—not just physical balance but balance in all things. The first rule a student learns is that the uniform belt (*obi*) is tied evenly on both sides; this represents balance in all aspects of life: job, family, social relationships, and religion.

Similarly, in negotiating we must maintain balance mentally and physically during a bargaining session. Practicing as often as possible makes us more aware of when our equilibrium is off because we're too aggressive or passive, too focused on ourselves or on the other party, too invested in the big-picture or the small-picture perspective. The best solutions are usually developed using a good balance of all your skills.

So when can you stop practicing? Never. Even for black belt martial artists, study never ends. They are always sparring, entering tournaments, observing others, watching videos, and more. In martial arts we strive for *kaizen*, which is a Japanese word meaning small but never-ending efforts to improve. Black belts will not settle for mediocrity. They recognize that each day there is only one chance to give their best, and constant practice provides that opportunity.

The same discipline is required to become a master negotiator. You must always think of money as a hard-won commodity, and all the products and services you need to buy and sell as an opportunity to earn more of it for yourself through kaizen. May this book be just the first step on your journey to becoming a black belt negotiator.

BLACK BELT TEST

Now it's time to test for the highest rank in negotiating, the black belt. To earn this honor, you must take all the skills you've learned and put them to use in a real-life situation, bargaining on a major purchase (more than $10,000). If you are not in the market for a car, boat, or house right now, find a friend who is and offer to negotiate on his or her behalf.

Once you have negotiated a big-ticket item, use the Belt Ranking Sheet in the appendix of this book to rate your negotiating skills. Don't expect to rank as a black belt on your first or even second try with a major purchase. Note where your scores are low, and look for another opportunity to improve. Don't give up until you do achieve black belt status on a regular basis.

Discipline means being consistent in your practice and your evaluation. You must rate yourself after every negotiation, no matter how big or small, regardless of whether money is involved or not.

Remember the indomitable spirit. Never give up and never forget that if you pass up an opportunity to negotiate, the answer will always be no.

Best of luck with all of your bargaining adventures!

APPENDIX

BELT RANKING SHEET

Rate yourself from 1 to 10 (10 is highest).

1. Developed rapport immediately   _____
2. Kept emotions under control   _____
3. Did not immediately talk about primary target _____
4. Flinched at proposals   _____
5. Shared information important to both parties   _____
6. Pointed out benefits to the other party _____
7. Used time effectively   _____
8. Developed time pressures   _____
9. Paced the other party   _____
10. Developed creative solutions   _____

TOTAL SCORE

90–100   **BLACK BELT:** You've mastered the art. Continue to improve.

80–89   **RED BELT:** You've developed advanced skills with control.

70–79   **BROWN BELT:** You've developed skills but without control.

60–69   **BLUE BELT:** You've mastered the basics.

50–59   **GREEN BELT:** You understand the basics.

40–49   **YELLOW BELT:** You see the power but have yet to experience it.

30–39   **WHITE BELT:** You are without knowledge.

Under 30   **UNRANKED:** You are seeking enlightenment.

NEEDS AND WANTS SHEET

NEEDS	WANTS

Certificate of Completion

This certificate attests to the fact on this date
_____, student _____
has completed the training necessary to earn a
Black Belt in negotiating. The above-named
student is entitled to all of the rights and
privileges accorded hereto. Student agrees to use
the acquired skills in an ethical manner at all
times for the benefit of all parties.

Michael Soon Lee

REFERENCES

Austin, L. 2000. *What's holding you back? 8 critical choices for women's success.* New York: Basic Books.

Babcock, L. and S. Laschever. 2003. *Women Don't Ask.* New Jersey: Princeton University Press.

Bazerman, M. and M. Neale. 1992. *Negotiating Rationally.* New York: Free Press.

Cardillo, Joseph. 2003. *Be Like Water: Practical Wisdom from the Martial Arts.* New York: Warner Books.

Cohen, Herb. 1980, *You Can Negotiate Anything.* NY: Bantam Books.

Dawson, Roger. 2001. *Secrets of Power Negotiating.* Franklin Lakes, NJ: Career Press.

Deshimaru, Taisen. 1982. *The Zen Way to the Martial Arts.* NY: Penguin Books.

Fisher, R. and W. Ury. 1981. *Getting to yes. Negotiating agreements without giving in.* New York: Houghton Mifflin.

Gladwell, M. 2000. *The tipping point: How little things can make a big difference.* New York: Little Brown.

Lawler, Jennifer. 2003. *Dojo Wisdom. 100 Simple Ways to Become a Stronger, Calmer, More Courageous Person.* New York: Penguin Compass.

Lee, Bruce. 1993. *Tao of Jeet Kune Do.* Burbank, CA: Ohara Publications.

Raifia, H. 1982. *The art and science of negotiation.* Cambridge, MA: Harvard University Press.

Ready, Romilla and Burton, Kate. 2004. *Neuro-Linguistic Programming for Dummies.* Foster City, CA: IDG Books.

Riley, Hannah C. and Babcock, Linda C., "Gender as a Situational Phenomenon in Negotiation" (September 2002). IACM 15th Annual Conference; and KSG Working Paper No. RWP02–037.

Tabata, Kazumi. 2003. *Secret Tactics: Lessons from the Great Masters of Martial Arts.* North Clarendon, VT: Tuttle Publishing.

INDEX